INTENSIVE
Coursebook 4

COUNTERPOINT

Mark Ellis & Printha Ellis

COUNTERPOINT INTENSIVE COURSE
developed from Counterpoint General English Course
is based on a short course syllabus devised by

STEPHEN KEELER
Educational Consultant for
THAMES VALLEY
CULTURAL CENTRES

Nelson

CONTENTS

In so many words

If you had been born in Glasgow you would probably speak English.

This street sign comes from Helsinki, and is an indication of the fact that seven per cent of Finns speak Swedish as their first language, and that quite a lot of the city's inhabitants are bilingual. Helsinki itself, however, isn't a bilingual or multilingual city, so it can't be compared with Singapore or Hong Kong, which definitely are. Nevertheless, it is an example of just how common multilingualism is in the world today. It is hard to believe, perhaps, in this shrinking world, that there are so many areas where people actively speak not just one language but two and sometimes three. Take India, for example. A Punjabi from the north and a Tamil-speaking Madrasi from the south will converse quite frequently in English, and the same Punjabi will also very likely speak Hindi. But it is in the world's border areas where multilingualism is chiefly found. Poor farmers on the Thai-Cambodian border are likely to speak two languages – Thai and Cambodian – but quite often they speak a third as well – Lao. The same is true for people living close to the Swiss borders, who might speak two or even three languages – German and French, perhaps, or French and Italian.

Some Africans might speak Arabic and French, while others might speak Swahili and English, and there are many Belgians who speak Flemish and French. If you go to Wales you'll find that there are Welsh who speak their own language at home and in the shops and English only when they have to, and the same is true for many other minority language groups in the world. In fact, the more one looks at the map, the more one realises that nationalities, although often monolingual over much of a territory, are also very often likely to be bilingual in certain areas.

The Americans, who pride themselves on being a nation which has developed out of such a varied background, are normally seen as a people with just one language – English. In fact, if you went into certain towns and certain areas of those towns, English wouldn't get you very far. If you spoke to a young child in the street you might not even get a word in reply. In areas of Miami, for example, the language is Spanish, and unless you were able to use that language freely you wouldn't be accepted.

Some people say that if an artificial language like Esperanto had been introduced and taught more widely then there would be no world-wide language problem today. Others say that no artificial language would be widely accepted and that people will always have a preference for the language of their birth. So it would still be true that if you had been born in Glasgow you would probably speak only English, whereas if you'd been born in Calcutta you'd speak Bengali and Hindi.

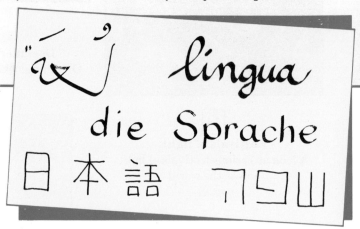

1 Read the text and decide whether the following statements are true or false.
1 Bilingualism means you speak many languages.
2 Punjabis speak Tamil.
3 People only speak Welsh at home.
4 People speak more than one language in some cities in the USA.
5 All Spanish-speaking people speak English in the USA.
6 The introduction of Esperanto would have solved all language problems.

2 Find words or expressions in the text which mean:
getting smaller   talk   mainly
something with many differences   invented

3 *Poor farmers on the Thai-Cambodian border are likely to speak two languages.* Look at the map and ask and answer questions, like this:
What languages are people living in ____/near the ____ border likely to speak? – I think that people living in/near ____ are likely to speak ____.

4 Work in pairs to build up a list of countries where the languages below are spoken. Ask and answer, like this:
Can you think of some countries where French is spoken? – Yes, it is spoken in ____ and ____.

French   English   Portuguese   Arabic   Chinese   Spanish

Now compare your list with other pairs, like this: *Where might you live if you spoke ____? – We might live in ____.*

5 *If you spoke to a child on the street you might not even get a word in reply.* Work in pairs to match the columns, and ask and answer questions, like this:
Why is Peter learning Arabic? – Well, he's going to visit ____, and he wouldn't/mightn't be able to ____ if he didn't learn the language.

A	B	C
Peter/Arabic	visit	read the street signs
Jane/French	teach	communicate very well
Dieter/English	study	do his/her job very well
Pablo/Chinese	do research	speak with his/her colleagues
Gordon/Russian	work	get a good job
Beatrice/Spanish	live	travel so easily

6 *If you had been born in Glasgow, you would probably speak only English.* Look at the map again and ask and answer about the towns, like this:
What would you speak if you had been born in ____? – I'd probably speak, or I might speak ____.

7 The six people below all wanted to get jobs in certain countries, but they were sent to different countries according to the language they spoke. Work in pairs, **A** and **B**. Complete the boxes by asking questions, like this: *Where would Wa be now if he hadn't spoken German/gone to Germany?*

Name	A		B	
	In	Would be	In	Would be
Wa	Germany		Australia	France
Ana		Austria		Scotland
Yvette	Spain		Brazil	
Liam		Greece		Chile
Pietro	Thailand		Belgium	
Medhat		New Zealand		

8 Listen to the tape. Someone is talking about the Welsh language.
1 The speaker says that at one time the English were very much against Welsh. Which words tell you this?
2 The speaker is not very happy with the situation at the moment. Which words tell you this?
3 The speaker is not against English. Which words tell you this?

Listen again and tick which word of these pairs of words you hear as you listen.

try   tried   encourage   discourage
aloud   allowed   wood   would

Do you think the speaker is very extreme or not? Find one or two sentences to support your conclusion.

GRAMMAR SUMMARY

Impossible condition (with present consequence)
If you'd been born in Glasgow, you'd probably speak only English.

Improbable condition
What might you speak if you were in . . . ?

9 Listen to the second speaker and complete these sentences:
1 I think you said that ____ better you ____ university.
2 If I ____, French for example, then maybe ____ job.
3 If ____ seventeen and eighteen, instead of having to earn money, it's ____ more confident.

Now write a sentence about yourself, talking about what you might now be able to do if you had done something when you were younger. Follow the example sentences above. Compare what you have written with other people, like this: *What did you say you might now be able to do? – I said that if I'd ____, I might/would now be able to ____.*

10 Try to think of a few more things that you regret (not) doing when you were younger, and think of the consequences. Are they present or past consequences? Write sentences, like this:
Present consequence: *If I had(n't) ____, I would/might now/be ____.*
Past consequence: *If I had(n't) ____, I would(n't) have done ____.*

11 Choose from the languages below to make sentences like this:
If I had the chance to speak another language it would be ____. (Write more than one sentence.)

Esperanto English Chinese Japanese Dutch German Spanish Portuguese Italian Swedish Hindi Russian Finnish

Now compare what you have decided with other people, like this:
What languages have you chosen? Why?

Now write a short paragraph saying what languages you have chosen and why, like this:
I chose ____ because I travel to ____ on holiday./. . . because I might need it for my work, etc.
Also say what languages would not be particularly useful for you, and give a reason.

1

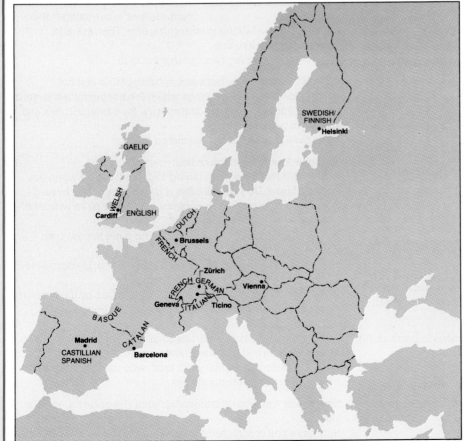

What do you call your parents? Mother? Father? Mum? Dad? Or perhaps you call them by their first names? These days, many young children do call their parents, and their parents' friends, by their first names, and yet there are also many countries where this kind of familiarity is very difficult and causes a lot of discomfort, especially among older people.

In some languages, French and German for example, there are two very precise forms for the word *you*. In German it is *du* for the familiar word and *Sie* for the more formal. In France, the familiar word is *tu*, and the more formal is *vous*. In English there is now only the one form, *you*, although a few hundred years ago there was also the more formal expression *thou*.

In Germany and France the two forms are very much part of everyday life. In Germany for example, it is still possible to find two people who have been working together for years still calling each other *Herr Schmidt*

and *Frau Müller*, not only in the place of work, but also outside in the street, or in each other's homes. In both countries it often isn't acceptable for an older person to be addressed by the word *du* or *tu* when talking to a younger person, or to someone junior at work, although in both countries the informal form is usually used by younger people when they are talking to each other. In contrast to this, neither an American nor an Australian has this difficulty, and in fact in the work situation English-speaking people quite often call each other by their first names.

In France, the use of the word *tu*, therefore, has a much more significant meaning than the use of the first name in English. In New Zealand when you are talking to another person there is no alternative. You've got to use the word *you*. In France, the sudden change from *vous* to *tu* shows a change in the relationship, from one which is quite formal to one which is much more familiar.

Call me mister!

1 Read the passage above and answer these questions.
1 Give two examples of the less formal *you* forms.
2 If you don't know someone very well in Germany what will you probably call them?
3 English did have a formal *you* form. What was it?

2 Find these words in the passage and replace them with one of the words in the box below: these days precise everyday significant alternative familiar

important	in modern times	daily
choice	casual	exact

Read the new sentence to your partner. Does he/she agree?

3 *In Germany . . . it is still possible to find two people who have been working together for years still calling each other Herr Schmidt and Frau Müller.* Work in pairs to make a list of things it is possible or impossible to find in your own town or country. Check with other groups, like this:
What have you decided is impossible to find in Paris?
– We've said that it's impossible to find a good ____./someone who ____.

4 What do you call each other? Ask questions in pairs about the people in the list below, like this:
Tell me what you and your father call each other.   – I call my father 'Dad' and he calls me ____/by my first name.

father mother grandmother grandfather your doctor best friend's father/mother your teacher the man/woman who runs the local shop

5 Some people find that it isn't acceptable to call others by their first names. Make lists of things which are unacceptable in your society (think about relationships with other people – in the home, on the street, when using public transport, when talking to strangers, etc). Then ask and answer in pairs, like this:
What do you think isn't acceptable for us in ____?

What is the difference between *not acceptable* and *not permitted*? Make lists of things which are not permitted in your country (think about laws – traffic laws, for example). Ask and answer in pairs, like this:
What have you said is not permitted in ____?

Now check with others, like this:
We've said that it's not permitted to cross the road when you see a red man. Do you think this is good or not?/We've said that it's unacceptable for people to ____. What have you said?

6 Write these sentences, completing them in your own words.
1 The French have two forms of the word *you*. In contrast to this ____.
2 Franz Böhm and Dettlef Stahl call each other by the familiar form. In contrast to this, their parents, the Böhms and Stahls, ____.
3 In contrast to Madame Brunaud and Monsieur Robert, who are very formal with each other, Jacques and Pierre ____.
4 ____ to Marcel and Marie Chantal, who use the *tu* form, Marie's grandparents always ____.

Now check with your partner. Ask what she or he has written, like this:
How have you completed the first sentence?   – I've said ____.

The English language may not have different words for *you*, like French or German, or some Oriental languages which have many more, but an Englishman walking into a business meeting will speak differently from an Englishman walking into a pub, for example. The language used will range from very formal to very familiar.

7   Listen to the tape and tick which level of formality applies to each conversation. Write where you think each conversation takes place.

	Very formal	Formal	Neutral	Familiar	Very familiar
1					
2					
3					
4					
5					
6					

Now listen again and try to decide why you chose these levels of formality. Discuss it in groups, like this:
I think number 1 is familiar because they use first names.
– Wouldn't you call it very familiar, then?

For some people the sudden change from the formal to the informal form can be so upsetting that they cannot accept it. For example, in a small German company there were about twenty people working in an office and most of these people had been working together for many years. All used the formal *Sie* form. Then one morning two of the men who had known each other socially for many years suddenly decided to use the *du* form at work. After work that day, the Director went up to one of the two men and asked him why he had started to use the *du* form with Herr Braun. This man, Conrad Weinmann, said that surely it didn't matter whether he used *du* or not. Herr Braun was still Herr Braun. The Director accepted the argument but insisted that they only use the *Sie* form at work.

GRAMMAR SUMMARY

Adjective + infinitive
It's impossible to find someone who . . .
It's not permitted to cross the road when you see a red man.

So* + adjective + *that
They are so formal that they use the *Sie* form.

Past perfect continuous
The people had been working together for many years.

8   *For some people the sudden change from the formal to the informal form can be so upsetting that they cannot accept it.* Match Columns **A, B** and **C**, then ask questions, like this:
What have you said about the Director?   – I've said that he was so formal that he couldn't accept 'du' at work.

A	B	C
the Director	traditional	use *tu* with each other
Braun and Weinmann	complex	accept *du* at work
older people (can be)	formal	use last names
some Oriental languages	formal	use *Mr* and *Mrs*
young people in France	friendly	call each other *du*
Victorian couples	informal	have many levels of formality

Now compare your information with other people.

9   In the small German company in the text, the people *had been working* together for many years. In pairs, build up a list of things they had been doing together for many years, like this:
They had been calling each other Sie.
. . . addressing the Director as Herr _____.
. . . eating lunch together, etc.

Also build up a list about Braun and Weinmann:
They had been seeing each other socially for some time/going to the pub . . . etc.

Now compare your list with other pairs.

10   In groups, talk about the people below, as in the example:
Peter/work/(town) (time) (job)
A   What can you tell me about Peter?
B   He's been working in Vienna for 20 years, and he's a doctor.
Now change partners and ask and answer like this:
A   What did your old partner tell you about Peter?
B   He said that Peter had been working in Vienna for 20 years and that he was a doctor.

Think of periods of time and jobs yourself.
1   Robert/work/Paris
2   Marie/work/Moscow
3   Alphonse/live/New York
4   Mario/study/Dublin
5   Patrick/study/Cambridge

11   It could be said that in an ideal world, levels of formality wouldn't matter. What do you think?

Work in groups. Choose one from each of these lists of characteristics (**A**) and rights that would be possible in an ideal world (**B**). Tell other groups what you have listed, like this:
Pedro, what has your group decided on?   – We think that in an ideal world it wouldn't matter if you were young or old, you could still _____.

A   young/old, black/white, man/woman, sick/healthy, rich/poor
B   get free medicine, go wherever you wanted, have a holiday every year, get the same pay, be respected by your neighbours, have the same opportunities.

2

A matter of MANNERS

When you start talking about good and bad manners you immediately start meeting difficulties. Many people just cannot agree what they mean. We asked one person, who replied that she thought you could tell a well-mannered person by the way they occupied the space around them – for example, when such a person walks down a street he or she is constantly aware of others. Such people always seem to walk into gaps. They don't bump into other people.

However, a second person thought that this was more a question of civilised behaviour than good manners. Instead, this other person told us a story, which he said was quite well known, about an American who had been invited to an Arab meal in one of the countries of the Middle East. The American hadn't been told very much about the kind of food he might expect. If he had known about Arab food, he might have behaved better. Immediately before him was a very flat piece of bread that looked, to him, very much like a napkin. Picking it up, he put it into his collar; so that it fell, like a napkin, across his shirt.

His Arab host, who had been watching, said nothing, but immediately copied the action of his guest.

And that, said this second person, was a fine example of good manners.

But is there really so much difference between the two examples? Both show concern for other people and a desire not to cause offence or embarrassment.

1 Read the text and say if the following are true or false.
1 It's difficult for people to agree what is meant by good manners.
2 The writer talks about an American he met in the Middle East.
3 The writer says he was not familiar with Arab food.
4 The Arab host was well mannered.
5 The incident was caused by an ignorance of another culture.

2 Complete the words from the text in Column **A**, then match them with definitions from Column **B**.

A	B
c _ _ sta _ _ ly	interest and awareness
g–p–	something to protect your clothes when you eat
n _ _ k _ _	empty spaces
cop _ _ d	all the time
con _ _ _ n	did the same action

3 The American didn't know much about Arab food and customs. *If he had known about Arab food, he might have behaved better.*
Put the verbs in these sentences in the correct tense to express ideas like the above.
1 If the American (know) more about Arab food, he (eat) the bread.
2 If the Arab (not have) such good manners, he (not copy) his guest.
3 If the Arab (not have) such good manners, he (laugh at) his guest.
4 If the American (realise) his mistake, he (be) very embarrassed.

4 Make sentences about manners from the table below, like this:
If ____ had known how to use chopsticks, ____ would have eaten more food.
If ____ had understood he/she should queue up, he/she would/might not have waited ____.

Peter Diana Pablo Kurt Tom Karen	know understand	more about how to he/she should	use chopsticks formal parties English food queue up be quiet say please	worn a suit/dress. had to leave the library. waited so long in the shop. eat more food. offended so many people. eat the meat pie.

5 What actions do you think are impolite or polite? Make a list, in groups, of five impolite and five polite actions.
For example:

impolite
talking loudly on the bus

polite
giving up your seat for an elderly person

Now ask other groups and build up a list of what they have written down, like this:
What was one thing that you thought was impolite? – *We said that talking loudly on the bus was impolite.*

A real problem with politeness is that an action which is polite in one country might not be seen as polite in another. For example, a westerner who has been asked to go out to a meal with a Chinese host may be given fried rice at the end of the meal. Now, the correct signal to show you do not want to eat any more – that you are full and have had enough – is not to finish the rice on the plate. However, the poor Englishman, or Frenchman, not wishing to seem impolite, finishes the rice, only to find to his embarrassment that his plate is full once again.

6   Listen to the tape and answer these questions:
1   How does the woman ask her friend if she wants some tea?
2   What does the friend say in reply?
3   How does the man ask his friend if he wants some more food?
4   What does his friend say in reply?
5   The man now repeats his original question, but very strongly. What does he say?

7   Roleplay
You are eating at someone's house, but you do not know them very well. Do the roleplay according to the instructions below.

A – You are the host. Offer your guest some more food.
B – You are the guest. Refuse politely.
A – Insist that your guest eats some more. You know he/she is only being polite in refusing.
B – You have had a very good meal. Explain to your host that you have eaten enough and can't eat any more.

8   In different countries there are very different customs concerning what people do when they meet for the first time, or when they meet on other occasions. Look at the list below, and in pairs decide <u>only</u> on what things you *need not* or *should not* do, when you meet for the first time, or meet on other occasions.
Make notes, like this:
bow to each other   *1st meeting = needn't…*
shake hands
ask about your family
ask about your health
kiss
stand very close

Now discuss the list with other groups, like this:
We've put that you needn't bow to each other on the first meeting.
– And you needn't kiss.
In our country you shouldn't kiss on the first meeting.

9   Listen to the pieces of conversation on the tape and make a note of the situation, then make sentences, like this:
If her guests had said thank you, she would have invited them again.

10   In pairs, think of a country (which you have visited) which has very different customs from your country. Make a list of things which happened to you in that country, like this:
I was stared at in the street.
I was asked if my hair was real.
I was given ____ to eat.
(Invent these if necessary.)

Discuss your lists in groups of four. Tell the other pair what happened to you. Make notes of what they say. Now try to guess which country they are talking about.

Finally, report back to the class about what happened to the other pair in your group, like this:
They said that they had been stared at in the street and that ____. Which country is it?

11   Here are some English proverbs.
Children should be seen and not heard.
Manners make the man.
People in glass houses shouldn't throw stones.
What do these mean? Do you agree? Do you know any other proverbs?

12   Listen to the tape. You will hear some people giving their opinions about good and bad manners.
As you listen complete the sentences, using the guidelines below:

First person
I think that when ____ ____ ____, then that is ____ ____.
If you're ____ ____ work, for example, and people ____ that ____ ____, then that's ____ ____.   I don't think it's really just a ____ of saying ____ or ____ ____.

Second person
If I find a woman ____ in ____ ____ or on the ____, then I certainly ____ her ____ ____.   Replying ____ to ____ and ____ ____. That's a sign of ____ ____.
Speaking ____ ____ and ____ ____ when no one else is interested. That's ____ ____ for me.

Third person
Helping ____ ____ with ____ ____. Asking ____ if she wants ____. That's ____ ____, isn't it?

Fourth person
I ____ people who ____ ____ the street with those ____ ____ on ____ ____.
And ____ who ____ on the ____ and ____.
Do you agree or disagree with each one?

3

SHRINKING WORLD

The world is getting smaller. People travel from one part of it to another in a matter of hours. And increasingly, men and women from different nationalities, cultures and races meet, marry and have children. This is a fact of life now; it will always continue to
5 be one. Mixed marriages are not something which one thinks about as strange any longer; they have become commonplace.

Strangely enough, however, when one talks to partners in mixed marriages, often it is not the very extreme example, such as a Japanese woman married to a British man, where one finds
10 complications and problems. Real problems of understanding can occur within the same language group, such as the British and Americans, or similar culture groups, such as the Scandinavians and the Germans.

We have spoken to several mixed couples and have come up with some rather surprising conclusions. When couples are from 15 very obviously different backgrounds, each person is very careful, or tends to be very careful, to try to understand what the other is saying or what the other person feels, or thinks. When there are apparent similarities, however, such as the same language or similar culture backgrounds, the couples tend to 20 assume they already understand each other, when in fact on very many different points they don't understand each other at all. This is what leads to problems.

1 Read the text. Say what these words refer to:
another (line 2)   it (line 4)
one (line 5)   the other (line 17/18)
this (line 23)

2 Find words which mean the following:
usual   take place   found   think

3 Answer these questions:
1 The author says, 'this is a fact of life now (line 4)'. What does he mean by this statement?
2 What is the first conclusion the author has come up with in paragraph 3?
3 What is the second conclusion in paragraph 3?

4 Match Columns **A** and **B**, and ask and answer questions, like this:

Can you tell me where/in which countries (continents) one finds ____? – ____ is/are found in ____./One can find ____ in ____.

A	B
problems with rainfall	North
high temperatures	America
low temperatures	Greenland
wild animals such as	Africa
kangaroos	India
polar bears	the Sudan
gorillas	Australia

5 Consider these situations, then choose from the ideas below and make sentences using *must be able to/should/shouldn't* or *have got to*.
Work in pairs, and make sentences like this:
If one marries someone who ____, one must be able to/has got to/should/shouldn't ____.
If one marries someone who:
1 comes from another culture
2 speaks another language
3 doesn't speak the language well
4 is not used to the climate

learn patience   tolerant   helpful
angry   impatient
help them understand their problems
try to explain the differences
learn theirs   learn about theirs
sympathetic

6 What kind of problems do you think a person in a mixed marriage might face? (For example, an Egyptian man married to a French woman.)
Think about these areas:

career choice/hours of work	the in-laws religion
holidays	attitudes to men
children, their education and upbringing	and women sense of humour

Think of some ideas, and then discuss them with a partner. You can use these phrases:
People might face problems, such as ____ ing ____.
There might be differences of opinion over ____ because ____.
Attitudes to ____ may differ, with the result that ____.
Now write a summary of your discussion.

David   **Madeleine**

7 You are going to hear two different people talking, both of whom have mixed marriages. They are David from England whose wife, Madeleine, is French and Peter, also English, whose wife, Mary Ann, is from the United States of America. Before you listen, work in pairs and build up a list of problems you think each couple will face.

Mary Ann

Peter

Ask questions, like this:
What about David and Madeleine? What kind of problems do you think they might have? Michel, have you got any ideas?
Now build up another list of advantages you think couples like this will enjoy.
What kind of advantages can you think of? What special benefits do you think this kind of marriage offers?

8 Now listen and note down the problems and advantages which you hear in each case. Do this by completing the following statements, and then decide whether each one is a problem or an advantage.

1 David says that he feels much ____.
2 He says that now he speaks ____.
3 He says that his life ____.
4 He says that at the beginning Madeleine used to ____.
5 He says that Madeleine thinks that ____.
6 He says that Madeleine doesn't like the way ____.
7 Peter says that to begin with he and Mary Ann ____.
8 He says that Mary Ann didn't understand ____.

9 He says that there's a great difference in ____.
10 He says that he's now got ____.

9 Listen to the tape again and complete these sentences, each of which includes the reflexive form ____ self/selves.
David: She'd just sit ____ French.
But I ____ think ____ just the same.
Peter: She's constantly concerned about ____.
You're good because ____, not because ____.

10 Draw comparisons between the likes/dislikes of your friends and relatives and your own, like this:
My mother hates staying up late, but/whereas I myself rather enjoy it.
Make sentences about the following:
staying up late   playing the piano
watching the news on TV   doing nothing
going round the shops   lying on the beach
studying English

4

Men and women ...

We have talked to three women, each in rather different circumstances, and looked at the way they manage their day-to-day affairs. Two are married, one of them with children. The other is a single parent.

It is Wednesday. Carol Dee arrives home at nine o'clock. It has been a long day. Early this morning she left Birmingham, where she had spent the night after a long meeting the previous day. Tomorrow morning she flies to Paris, where quite a lot of her store's dress collection will be bought. By the end of the week she will have clocked up over 70 hours, including travel time.

Richard, her husband, is out. She knows he's been back already from work because the television is on. But he's cooked his meal and done the washing up. Good old Richard.

She looks at her watch. Nine-twenty. She wonders where he is. He often leaves a note.

It occurs to her that it's quite likely she'll be asleep when he returns. These days they hardly see each other at all.

She makes herself a cup of tea. She's too tired to eat. It's 3rd March. She looks at the calendar on the kitchen wall and remembers there has been talk of sending her to Brussels. She sits down and wonders when she's going to be told.

5

> **Subject**
>> Carol Dee
>
> **Age**
>> 29
>
> **Profession**
>> Buyer for a large department store in London.
>
> **Status**
>> Married. No children. Husband is a solicitor.

1 Read the text and answer the questions.
1 How many cities are mentioned?
2 What does she have for her evening meal?
3 There is something Richard has not done. What is it?
4 Do you think she minds that Richard isn't at home?

2 Now complete these sentences:
1 Carol Dee is a ____ who ____.
2 Richard and Carol ____.
3 Their relationship seems to be ____.
4 Carol works ____.

3 Which of these things do you do when you get home from work?
1 Make yourself a cup of tea, coffee or something else.
2 Make yourself a sandwich. What kind?
3 Pour yourself a long, cold drink. Of what?
4 Cook yourself a nice, hot meal.
Work in pairs and ask and answer questions. Use the word(s) *myself/ourselves* and these words *sometimes/often/like to*:
What do you do when you get home? – I often make myself a cup of tea.

> **Subject**
>> Suzanne Miller
>
> **Age**
>> 34
>
> **Profession**
>> Housewife
>
> **Status**
>> Married. Three children. Husband is a metal worker.

Most of the time Suzanne's tired. If they had a new vacuum cleaner she'd be happier, but Peter says they can't afford it. It's always money. She's more tired now than she used to be, but then she's not sleeping very well. Of course, there's the youngest child, Paul. That must be it, he never seems to sleep. Six months old now. Peter doesn't seem to have any problem sleeping. Last night, for example he came home at six, turned on the TV and fell asleep. It must have been

because he was exhausted after a hard day's work. But does he really work as hard as she does? He must do, she tells herself. Otherwise, how can he sleep like that?

Her other two children are nine and eight. Both at school. By the time she's got them off in the morning, come back, made the beds and cleaned up after them, Paul has woken up and is crying. She often wonders what would happen if she weren't there. What would Peter do then?

Peter is at home at lunchtime and expects a hot meal, and another hot meal in the evening. Somewhere during the day she manages to get the shopping done. If she had the car it would be easier. But of course, she hasn't got it. Peter needs it.

4 Complete these statements in your own words.
1 One of the problems seems to be ____.
2 Another seems to be ____.
3 Suzanne feels ____.
4 Peter is someone who ____.

5 Work in pairs.
1 Choose two words to describe Suzanne and find a sentence in the text to support each choice.
idle   quiet   hardworking
exhausted   bored   happy
2 Find a sentence which tells you the husband does not eat at work.
3 Find sentences in the text which tell you there are three children.

6 Work in pairs. Match Columns **A** and **B**, and then ask and answer, like this:
I wonder why Peter is so tired?   –It must be because he's had a hard day.

A	B
Peter/tired	eat something bad
Jane/pleased	argue with her husband
Bob/angry	have a hard day
Karen/upset	lose a lot of money
Gary/ill	get a better job

7 Why did Peter fall asleep in front of the TV? – *It must have been because he was exhausted.*
Suzanne wasn't absolutely sure about this but it seemed the most likely explanation. Work in pairs, and ask and answer questions about these people.
1 Peter/get a taxi
2 Bill/fail his exam
3 Jean-Claude/go to bed early
4 Katrina/go/shops
5 Jacques and Pierre/miss/plane

▶ **Subject**
▶▶ Katherine Dolby

▶ **Age**
▶▶ 32

▶ **Profession**
▶▶ Teacher

▶ **Status**
▶▶ Single Parent. Two children.

'I think that I split up with David because he didn't appreciate what I wanted from our marriage. I didn't want to spend all my time in the house, and I certainly didn't want to spend it all in the kitchen. Anyway, that's over now.

I teach at a secondary school about a mile away. I walk, of course. There's no money for a car. I'm a maths teacher and I enjoy my work, although I find that the fifteen and sixteen-year-olds that I deal with often don't really care. I mean, most of them are going to be unemployed, anyway.

I've got two children. A neighbour takes them off with her kids in the morning to the primary school. They have their lunch there, so I don't have to bother about that. Then, in the afternoons they come back home about five.

It's not easy with the children. They want to bring their friends round in the evening when all I want is a bit of peace and quiet. There doesn't seem to be much time for anything, really.'

8 Answer these questions about Katherine and her family.
1 Give one reason why the marriage split up.
2 What is Katherine's job?
3 Who takes her children to school in the morning?
4 Where do the children eat their lunch?

9 Find words in the text which mean: separate   understand   work with children   worry about

10 A man's role?
What do you think a man's role should be in the house? Decide what he should do in these two situations:
no children, husband and wife both work
two children, wife doesn't work outside the home
Make sentences beginning *A man should _____*.

11 Listen to Richard, Carol Dee's husband, talking to an interviewer.
1 Complete these questions/statements from the tape.
She must _____.
Does that _____?
Doesn't it_____?
2 The interviewer's last question is unanswered. In pairs, decide on a suitable reply.

3 Using the information from Carol Dee and from her husband, write a short paragraph describing the kind of relationship they have.

Now listen to Katherine Dolby's ex-husband talking to the interviewer.
4 Complete these sentences:
Go _____.
Didn't she _____?
It must have _____.
5 There are two very opposite points of view from these two people. Decide what they are, and then write a short paragraph, using these words:
although   however   on the other hand

12 In pairs, think of some questions you would like to ask Suzanne Miller, and some to ask her husband. Ask and answer in pairs, interviewing first Suzanne and then her husband.

5

... women and men

THE NATURAL WAY
Helping you to help yourself

At the Natural Way Clinic we believe that the body heals itself naturally, unless this healing process is blocked. We offer the services of professional practitioners of natural medicine who can help to unblock the body's own healing power. Although natural medicine can be used to treat specific symptoms, such as chronic headache, it concentrates on the individual as a whole, to make you feel better and healthier all over.

So read the descriptions of some of the natural approaches we offer; one of them may well be right for you.

HEALING

Healing by touch or thought without any medical help is still not generally accepted, but there is little doubt that it can work.

We still retain some examples of it in our everyday lives. In the event of a child having a temperature, we know that sometimes we can calm him or her by smoothing the brow. Then the fever may go down and the child will be able to sleep, giving the body the opportunity to fight the illness. We also all know people who respond better to one doctor than another. We say these doctors have a good 'bedside manner'.

The laying on of hands is probably the oldest and simplest form of healing. It is merely a reaction between two or more people. The healer and subject seem to set up an exchange of energy which speeds up the patient's own internal healing processes.

If you do not believe in healing, it doesn't mean that it won't work. Nearly everyone who comes to us does so as a last resort – because they are ill and are not responding to orthodox treatment. Healing works regardless of beliefs, and personal experience is more valuable than theory.

1   Read the explanation of healing above and find sentences which contradict the statements below.
1   Healing by touch does not work.
2   Healing is a complex form of treatment which no one understands.
3   Healing often doesn't work because people don't believe in it.

2   Find a word or words in the text which mean the following:
to make better   stroking the forehead when nothing else will work
treatment that is common and accepted

Now find one or more examples of the following: a symptom
a natural approach   a form of healing

3   There is an expression in the text which means *if*. What is it?
Look at these signs. Where do you think they come from? Ask and answer questions in pairs, like this:
Where do you think you might see the first sign?   – I think I'd see it on a ____.

Make sentences about the signs using *in the event of* and *in case of.*
Now, with your partner, write one or two warnings, using *in the event of* and *in case of*, and read them to the class. Can they guess the situation?

4   A well-known healer is being interviewed about his first experience of healing, but we can't hear what the interviewer is asking him. Which of the sentences below best describe the healer's attitude to healing? (You can choose more than one.)
He doesn't believe in healing.
He feels healing is natural for him.
He feels pain when he is healing.
He thinks healing can be embarrassing.

Now listen to the tape again and complete the questions below with the words you think the interviewer used.
1   How long have ____?
2   Did someone ____?
3   Did you know ____?
4   What exactly ____?
5   Do the people ____?
6   Can the healers ____?
7   Has it ever ____?

Listen to what the interviewer actually said. How close were you?

5   These sentences are from the tape: *I didn't even think about what I was doing. It must have been because there wasn't time.* He guessed that lack of time was the reason for his action.
Look at the reasons below and write a list of actions. Then read one of your actions to your partner, who guesses the reason, like this:
She saw 'Close Encounters of the Third Kind' seven times.   – It must have been because she liked it.

It must have been because he/she didn't have enough money.
It must have been because there wasn't time.
It must have been because they'd seen each other before.
It must have been because they hadn't seen each other for years.
It must have been because there was a hole in it.
It must have been because it didn't work.
It must have been because he/she liked it.

Now use your own reasons to write sentences, like this:
If she hadn't liked the film, she wouldn't have gone to see it seven times.

6

6 Column **A** lists things which have happened. Column **B** lists possible reasons. Match the two columns and check with your partner, like this: *The telephone rang at 3 a.m. last night.* – *It must have been your cousin from Brazil.*

A	B
The phone rang at 3 a.m.	cousin from Brazil
I felt ill last night.	a thief
Someone stole my wallet.	the recurring illness
Someone sent Alice a bunch of roses.	the man in the office
Pierre was rushed to hospital yesterday.	the seafood
Someone borrowed the car without asking.	a friend or relative
Someone broke the lock on the door.	her boyfriend

7 The healer says that he wouldn't have known that he could heal unless he'd done it in the war. Look at the actions of the people below and write why they happened for three of them. Then talk to your partner, like this:
I'm surprised she stayed in Canada for five years. – *Well, she wouldn't have stayed unless she'd liked it.*
Angela left her husband after 20 years.
Robert rushed off without saying goodbye.
Yvette married someone 20 years older.
Marie and Guillaume had seven children.
Russell refused the offer of a free flight to Hong Kong.
Barbara went on a crash diet.

8 Write down a list of medicines which you or your family have been given by a doctor (or have bought) in the past year, and give it to two other people. They guess why you have taken them, like this:
I think she must have bought the aspirins because she had a toothache. – *I don't agree. I don't think she'd have taken them unless she'd had a headache.*

9 One of the sensations people feel when touched by a healer is like pins and needles. Can you think of other times when you might feel like that? Here are some more expressions which describe pain or body sensations: I felt like I was burning up, my hair stood on end, my foot was asleep, my stomach was churning, my heart stopped, I was chilled to the bone, my mouth was on fire.
List when and why people experience such sensations, and discuss them.

HYPNOTHERAPY

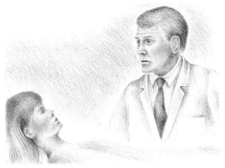

Hypnotherapy helps people to overcome a variety of problems such as smoking, insomnia, phobias or lack of confidence. We help people to help themselves. You can't be made to do or say anything you don't wish to say or do. Hypnotherapy is absolutely safe and natural and many doctors and dentists now use it.

When you are physically and mentally relaxed your subconscious mind is free to accept suggestions for replacing an old, and bad, habit with a new and better one. For example, the smoker sees himself refusing a cigarette and saying 'No thanks, I don't smoke.'

SHIATSU

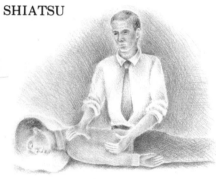

Shiatsu has been used as a simple remedy in the Orient for centuries. In Japanese, *shiatsu* means 'finger pressure'. It usually involves applying firm pressure to various points on the skin. These are mainly the ones used in acupuncture, so Shiatsu is often referred to as acupressure. Shiatsu therapy can help the body to heal itself. However, it is important first to reduce the intake of processed food and drinks, and to maintain a healthy, balanced diet of natural foods.

In Oriental medicine it is said that any illness or symptom, such as asthma, migraine or depression, is caused by the imbalance of a person's vital energy and this must be rebalanced to restore health. This energy travels through the body in twelve pathways known as meridians. By massaging the meridians, a proper balance can be re-established.

10 Read the descriptions of healing, hypnotherapy and shiatsu, and decide which one(s) these statements refer to.
1 It helps people to help themselves.
2 It is an old and simple form of healing.
3 It is similar to acupuncture.
4 It is not a Western form of medicine.
5 It is dependent on the reaction between patient and 'doctor'.
6 It is not generally accepted.

11 What do you think of alternative medicine?
In groups, look at the list of treatments below and discuss which should be paid for by the government, paid for by the individual, or which should be banned.
transplants   open heart surgery
acupuncture   hypnotherapy
chiropractic   healing   shiatsu
homeopathic medicine   herbal medicine
psychiatric treatment

12 Write a letter to your Member of Parliament (or other Government representative), and explain why you feel that certain treatments should/shouldn't be paid for by the Government. Begin like this:
Dear ____
I feel very strongly that the National Health Service/the Government should/shouldn't pay for ____ because . . .

GRAMMAR SUMMARY

Impossible condition
She wouldn't have stayed unless she'd liked it.
She wouldn't have taken them unless she'd felt ill.

Must have
It must have been because there wasn't time.

In the event of/in case of
In the event of a child having a temperature . . .

Salt, sugar and fat are things we are all careful about when we choose our food. Nevertheless, these days people are much more anxious about additives – special substances which are added to food for a number of reasons, for example, to improve the flavour, or add more colour.

Most of these additives have a number. Many of the numbers have an E in front of them. Some of these E numbers are colours, some are preservatives, others are thickeners, or sweeteners.

The E in E numbers stands for the EEC (The European Economic Community), which had already started to look at the problem of additives before the UK became a member in 1973.

The EEC intends to establish a list of additives which are acceptable, and which it can allow in member countries. However, it won't have completed the list for some time, and many additives are still without a number. If an additive has no E before the number, it may mean that the EEC has rejected it.

What's the problem?

Much of our food today is not natural, but processed, and processed food contains additives. The average Briton, born in 1980, will have eaten about 50 kilos of additives by the year 2000.

After Maurice Hanssen's book *E is for Additives* had set out the possible effect of additives on certain users, it was thought that some additives might cause certain people to feel unwell, or suffer from allergies and even nervous disorders, and that they can cause children to behave in abnormal ways.

FOOD FOR THOUGHT

1 Read the text and say whether the following statements are true or false.
1 All additives improve colour and flavour.
2 All additives have an E number.
3 When the UK joined the EEC, the EEC started to build a list of additives.
4 Now the list of additives is complete.
5 Not all people suffer from the effects of additives.

2 Find words in the text which mean:
concerned   make . . . better   taste
permit   not accepted   odd

3 Complete these sentences in your own words.
1 Although many people today are very worried about salt, sugar and fat in their food, they ____.
2 Additives which do not have an E before the number ____.
3 Britons born in 1980, within the first 20 years of their lives, ____.
4 Eating food with additives can ____.

4 *The average Briton, born in 1980, will have eaten about 50 kilos of additives by the year 2000.* Match Columns **A** and **B,** then ask and answer questions, like this:
What do you think the EEC will have done by the year 2000?   – I think it will have ____.

A	B
the United Nations	land/on Mars
the EEC	introduce/a world language
the British and the French	stop/using nuclear power
the Western Countries	solve/the problem of hunger
the Africans	build/the Channel Tunnel
the Russians	remove/all European frontiers
the USA	complete/the list of additives

Now discuss your statements with other pairs, like this:
What do you think about the EEC?
– We think it will have ____.
We agree./ We don't think it will have done that./It might have done that but it will have ____.

DID YOU KNOW THAT A GOOD DINNER COULD CONTAIN AT LEAST 72 ADDITIVES?

5 Write down six things you are doing at the moment, some long-term, some short-term. Decide which ones you will have completed/finished doing by the end of next week, and which you won't have completed. Then ask and answer in pairs, like this:
Tell me something that you will have/won't have finished by the end of next week.   – I will/won't have finished _____ing the _____.

Here are some suggestions to help you:
clean the house   paint the living room (kitchen etc.)
cut the grass   learn to drive   prepare for the party
write to my friend   arrange my holiday   study for my exam

6 Work in pairs. Make an outline of the days and dates of the next two weeks, like this:
Monday 7th July
Tuesday 8th July

Student **A**: Choose three evening activities (e.g. play, concert, meal out etc.) and choose which days to go. Write them down, invite **B** to come with you and ask why he/she can't come if he/she refuses. You start the conversation.
Student **B**: Choose three activities and write them next to days on your plan, to show when you are going to do them (one activity can last for two or three days). You cannot go out on these days until these three things are finished. Answer **A**'s questions, explaining if necessary, like this:
I can't come to _____ because I won't have finished _____.

7 Ask questions about the following abbreviations, like this:
Do you know what _____ stands for?   – Yes, doesn't it stand for _____?
BA   TWA   USA   USSR   UK   GB   UN   Co   Ltd   Mrs
Mr   Ms

8 Listen to the tape and answer the questions below. A woman is describing how additives affected her son, Robert.
1 Find expressions on the tape to describe Robert's behaviour.
2 Name four items of food the diet excludes.
3 How long has he been on the diet?
4 Summarise the problem with Robert.

9 Listen to the tape again and complete these sentences:
1 . . . he might be allergic to certain additives and he _____.
2 You really think it _____.
3 . . . the main problem _____.
Now write down the sentence which means:
Maybe I worried too much about him before.

10 Read through the following information about the E additives. Then ask and answer in pairs, like this:
I've got a terrible headache and I can't think why.   – You might have eaten some food containing E281.
My daughter is having very bad breathing problems.   – She might have eaten something which contains E102.

Now think of other reasons, like this:
I've got a terrible headache   – You might have drunk too much/stayed in the sun for too long.

```
E 290
function:  food preservative, coolant
possible side effect:  increase in
  absorption of liquid in the stomach,
  increasing the effect of alcohol.

E 281
function:  food preservative
possible side effect:  migraine headaches

E 250
function:  food preservative
possible side effects:  nausea, dizziness,
  low blood pressure.  These additives are
  prohibited for sale in foods for babies
  and young children.

E 249
function:  food preservative
possible side effect:  asthma

E 220
function:  food preservative
possible side effect:  irritation of the
  stomach

E 102
function:  colouring (yellow)
possible side effects:  skin rashes, hay
  fever, breathing problems
```

One of the noticeable effects of public concern is the reaction of the food industry – the suppliers and sellers of food. This concern was first noticeable in the US, with an increase in health food sales from 170 million dollars in 1970 to two billion dollars in 1981, but it soon spread to Europe.

In spite of the obvious effort involved, many UK supermarkets, including Tesco, Sainsbury and Safeway, have taken major steps. The latter has published its own booklet, listing the additives, and promising to remove many of them from its foods. The booklet mentions possible symptoms and indicates that some additives could lead to serious illness. However, the company also points out that, in spite of the fact that it will remove 51 different additives from its products, there is unlikely to be a great rise in cost.

11 Group survey
First read through the text and find the sentences with *in spite of* and *in spite of the fact that*. Then find out what food people in your group like to eat, and whether other people think it is bad for them, like this:
What food do you like?
– Hamburgers.
I think they're bad for you because they contain a lot of fat. (sugar/calories/preservatives/artificial colouring etc).

Now write some sentences about the other people in the survey, using the words *in spite of/in spite of the fact that*, like this:
Louis likes hamburgers in spite of | their fat content.
| the fact that they contain a lot of fat.

GRAMMAR SUMMARY

Future perfect
The EEC won't have completed the list for some time.
The average Briton will have eaten 50 kilos of additives by the year 2000.

***Might have* + past participle**
You might have stayed in the sun for too long.

In spite of (the fact that)
Louis likes hamburgers in spite of their fat content.

7

PARADISE LOST?

Christopher Columbus said that he had never seen anything so beautiful, trees 'beautiful and green, different from ours, with flowers and fruits . . . and little birds which sing very sweetly.'

The great navigator's impression, recorded in the journal of his voyage on 28th October 1492, is the first known written description of a rainforest. It remains hard to beat. Rainforests are, quite simply, extraordinarily beautiful. But the beauty is fragile.

Forty-five million years ago rainforest covered the city of London, and rainforests were then over 30 million years old. That makes them the oldest communities of living things on the planet.

Today the world's rainforests contain more than 50 per cent of the earth's living species, even though they cover no more than seven per cent of its surface. The greatest and most famous rainforest of all is found in Brazil, whose Amazon Basin, with its thousands of small and large streams, is almost totally covered by trees. The rest of the world's rainforests can be found in West Africa, South-East Asia, and the Pacific islands.

The forests live. A typical patch of rainforest, only four miles square, contains as many as 1,500 species of plant, 750 species of tree, 400 species of bird, 150 species of butterfly, 100 species of reptile, and 60 species of amphibian. The number of insects is so great that no one has been able to count them.

And yet this extraordinary powerhouse rests on poor foundations.

1 Read the text above and answer these questions:
1 How old are the rainforests?
2 What does the writer say about Columbus' description of the rainforests?
3 Name two places where you can find rainforests.
4 Name four kinds of living thing one can find in rainforests.
5 Why are these rainforests called a *powerhouse?*

2 Find words in the text which mean: can easily be broken   the remainder   small area   kinds

3 The passage mentions butterflies, as an example of one of the insects you can find in the forests. Match Columns **A** and **B** below to make definitions, like this:
A butterfly is an insect with brightly-coloured wings which flies.

A	B
parrot	insect/brightly coloured wings/flies
butterfly	small amphibian/jumps and makes loud noises
monkey	reptile/bites and crawls on the ground
papaya	bird/bright feathers/flies and talks
snake	mammal/long arms/lives in the trees
frog	fruit/orange flesh/grows in the tropics

In pairs write definitions for the things below, and then compare your definitions with other people. Use a dictionary if necessary.
tiger   spider   banana   eagle   orchid   pineapple

When the rainforests are cleared they take a long time to come back. A few rapidly growing species quickly become established, but this secondary growth, as it is called, is far less rich and varied. Large areas around Angkor Wat in Cambodia, cleared 600 years ago, still have not regained their former richness.

The modern world has speeded up the process. Once, it used to take a team of men a whole day to cut down a giant tree. Now, a single man can do it in ten minutes. The problem is that a single rainforest tree can be worth up to $1,000 in immediate sales. By the time it ends up in luxury furniture, this one tree may have made up to $17,000. Since 1945 half of the world's rainforests have come down.

It is people themselves who are the biggest cause of destruction. The wealthy own the best land, and the poor of the world are forced to find land where they can find it – and it is there, under the trees. So the trees are removed. When trees disappear from the land, the water sources suddenly disappear. The land itself washes away, either becoming very poor or complete desert. Worse still, the climate is likely to change as the trees are no longer there to absorb the carbon dioxide in the atmosphere. The gas rises and traps the sun's heat in much the same way as the glass of a greenhouse, leading to a slow but steady build up of temperature.

In the years to come perhaps people will say that much of our rainforest needn't have been destroyed. If the people of the world hadn't been so careless of their environment in the past, there would still be many large areas of rainforest left today, and so much of the planet's resources wouldn't have disappeared. After discovering what was happening, surely the countries most directly involved could see that something needed to be done.

Perhaps they did see.

4 *If the people of the world hadn't been so careless . . . so much of the planet's resources would not have disappeared.* Match the actions in Column **A** with the positive and negative consequences in **B** and talk in pairs, like this:
Diego, what would have happened if the people hadn't been so careless? . – If the people hadn't been so careless, so much of the planet's resources wouldn't have disappeared.

A	B
Angkor Wat/be/cleared people/be/so careless people/want/luxury furniture trees/disappear/from the land seas/be/overfished in the past land/become/desert people/want the land value of the rainforests/ understand	no one would now try to protect them they would not have had to cut down the trees so much of the planet's resources would not have disappeared the area around it would be much richer today it could be used to support crops and animals today so many trees would not have been cut down many countries would have a better fishing industry today the water sources would still be there

5 Work in groups. Think of actions and consequences in your own life and build up a list about your group by asking questions, like this:
Germaine, can you tell me about some important actions and consequences in your life? – Yes, if I hadn't left school so early I might/would have gone to university. – Yes, if I hadn't met Roger I would have married Pierre.
Now report to the class, by repeating one or more of the consequences you have heard.

6 *People will say that much of the land needn't have been destroyed.* Match Columns **A**, **B** and **C** to make sentences, like this:
I think that the rainforests needn't have been destroyed. What do you think should have been done? – I think they should have stopped cutting down the trees.

A	B	C
rainforests/destroy lakes and rivers/pollute buildings in the city/ make so dirty some African countries/ make so poor some towns/become so dangerous wild animals/become so rare	stop control improve	the use of coal in the cities the spread of poisonous chemicals cutting down the trees people hunting them the use of the land the living conditions of the people

7 Listen to the tape and complete the sentences below, which give advantages for human beings from the rainforests.
1 In 1960 ____ leukemia ____. Now ____. The reason for this is medicine from the ____ periwinkle, a ____, which the tribal ____ had ____.
2 The United States has found more than ____ with an ability to ____. More than ____ per cent of all drugs in the United States today have some connection with ____.
3 Other ____ include quinine, which comes from ____. People who suffer from high ____ get relief from ____.
4 There are also many new ____ in the ____, such as ____.
5 We use products everyday from ____, including ____. Today only ____ per cent of forest plants have been ____ for their potential.

8 Work in two groups, A and B. Read the information below.
A Read the two texts. Make a note of the reasons for the disappearance of the rainforests and add others of your own, e.g. building roads.

B Read the list of advantages you have written down from the tapescript in Exercise 7. Build up a series of arguments for saving the rainforests.

Now exchange information, like this:
B *What have you said is a reason for the disappearance of the rainforests?*
A *Well, one reason is that ____.*

A *What have you said is a good argument for saving the rainforests?*
B *Well, one reason is ____/another is ____.*

Now write a paragraph, either giving reasons for the rainforests' disappearance, or giving reasons for saving them.

9 Work in groups to build up a few arguments for cutting down the forests. Write a letter from someone who owns a logging company to a newspaper, defending his right to cut down trees.

8

GRAMMAR SUMMARY

Impossible condition
If the people of the world hadn't been so careless . . . so much of the planet's resources would not have disappeared.

Should have/needn't have
The rainforests needn't have been destroyed.
They should have stopped cutting down the trees.

ACID RAIN

WHAT IS 'ACID RAIN'?

Acid rain occurs when pollutants in the atmosphere, such as sulphur dioxide (SO_2) and nitrogen oxides (NO_x) react together. Polluted air can also contain gases which do direct damage or which react with other substances.

Norway's national bird is the dipper. It is found throughout the country and pays little attention to the ice and snow. The bird enjoys the freezing waterfalls and rapids of the country's rivers, and indeed that is where it finds its food.

Up until now there has been little threat to its existence, but recent research suggests that it may well be at risk from acid rain. Similar situations have been found in Great Britain and other countries too.

One of the effects of acid rain is the release of metals such as aluminium from the soil and riverbeds. Toxic substances are absorbed by the creatures that form the diet of the dipper, and therefore the bird builds up increasing amounts of toxic material in its body. As a result, the shell of its eggs becomes extremely thin, and because of that the eggs break.

If it cannot reproduce, how long can this national bird survive?

1 Find words in the text which mean: takes place   for example   danger   life   poisonous   quantities   very   continue to live

2 Ask and answer these questions in pairs.
1   Is the dipper worried by cold water?
2   Where does the dipper find its food?
3   What does acid rain release from the soil?
4   How does the dipper build up poison in its body?
5   What is the effect of this poison?

3 Look for these expressions in the text:
one of the effects is   therefore
as a result   because of that
Now complete these sentences, using these expressions. Student **A** should complete numbers 1 and 2, and Student **B** numbers 3 and 4. When you have finished, ask what the other person has said, and write down his/her sentences, like this:
What did you say about acid rain?
1   Acid rain releases ___. As a result, these substances ___.
2   Small creatures eat ___. Because of that ___.
3   The dipper eats ___. One of the effects is ___.
4   The eggshells of the dipper ___, and therefore ___.

4 Complete these situations in your own words.
1   In some parts of Africa it doesn't rain for years. As a result, ___.
2   Many people eat the wrong kinds of food. Because of that ___.
3   Acid rain falls on the forests and lakes of Scandinavia. As a result, ___.
4   Animals can't find the right kind of food. Therefore ___.
5   One of the effects of pollution is ___.
Now compare what you have written with your partner, like this:
What have you said for the first sentence?
– I've said that ___.

More than 300,000 tonnes of sulphur fall on Norway every year, almost 90% of this coming from other countries. The map shows the main sources of this in thousands of tonnes. The single biggest source is Great Britain. A further 103,000 tonnes comes from unidentified sources.

5 The caption on the left says that 90% of sulphur that falls on Norway comes from other countries. Look at the map, which shows which countries most of the pollution comes from. Each number refers to thousands of tonnes of sulphur. Ask and answer questions about the countries below, using these words: almost   just under   more than   approximately
What does the map tell us about the amount of sulphur falling on Norway from Sweden?
– It tells us that more than 300,000 tonnes fell on the country, with just under 10,000 tonnes coming from Sweden.
Can you give me the exact figure?
– Yes, the exact figure is ___.
Great Britain   Poland   Norway
East Germany   West Germany   Sweden

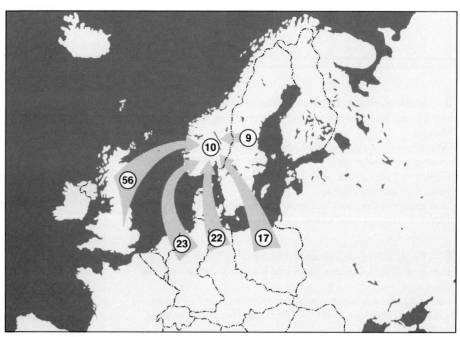

6 There is very little in the world not affected by acid rain. Read the text, then work in pairs and ask each other questions about these things:

rivers fish soil animals humans
trees buildings

Can you tell me from the text how ____ is/are affected by acid rain?

SOME OF THE MOST STRIKING EFFECTS OF ACID RAIN ARE:

● Water becomes acid and the concentration of toxic materials in rivers and lakes increases.
● Fish are poisoned and killed. Birds and animals which eat fish have no food, and this makes them leave their natural areas.
● Acid groundwater removes vital minerals essential for plant growth.
● Toxic substances become concentrated in land animals.
● People are directly affected by local pollution and by acid drinking water.
● Air pollution causes direct damage to forests. Trees weakened by acid rain could easily be damaged by strong winds, disease, and cold weather.
● Buildings, statues and monuments are damaged due to gases and acid rain.

7 Match Columns **A** and **B** and ask and answer questions, like this:
What have you said about poisoned food?
– We've said that it makes birds and animals leave their natural areas.

Use these verbs: make cause remove increase affect

A
poison in the dipper's food
acid groundwater
pollution from cars
acid rain
local pollution

B
important minerals from the soil
damage to buildings and cars
trees weak
people's health
the level of poison in rivers
the eggshell very thin and weak

8 *Trees weakened by acid rain could easily be damaged by strong winds.* Think of your own country. Make sentences from the chart, thinking of suitable things to fill the gap.

In the next ten years, ____	could be will be should be shouldn't be won't be	built developed improved damaged eliminated

Work in groups. Ask each other questions, like this:
Manuel, what do you think will be done in Spain in the next ten years? – I think the train service will be improved.

9 Write a short paragraph, commenting on the views of your group. Use these expressions/words:
however also on the other hand
____ thinks/feels that ____.
Manuel's opinion is that ____. However, he thinks that ____.

10 Listen to a report that appeared in the British media on March 17, 1986, and answer these questions.
1 What is Mrs Surlien about to do?
2 What do the Nordic countries feel?
3 What is Britain's reaction?
4 What were the Swedes responsible for?
5 What is the 30s club?
6 What is the Norwegian position?

Complete these sentences:
1 All the Nordic countries ____ deposit falling in southern Scandinavia.
2 Emissions from ____.
3 I don't see ____ live with.

11 At the time of this report Britain said it was not responsible for acid rain in Norway. You are members of the Scandinavian countries. Work in groups and decide on strong measures you will take to try to persuade Britain to change her mind. Choose from the following, or add another measure of your own:
make it more difficult for British people to enter Scandinavia
make it more difficult for British companies to export to Scandinavia
withdraw from all sports in Britain
get the United Nations to tell Britain to control pollution

When you have decided, exchange information with other groups, like this:
We've decided that ____. What have you said?

12 Based upon your decisions in Exercise 11, write a letter explaining your views to a national newspaper.

9

GRAMMAR SUMMARY

Expressions of consequence
As a result, the shell of its eggs becomes thin.

Present simple passive
Can you tell me how rivers are affected by acid rain?

Modal passive
Trees weakened by acid rain could easily be damaged by strong winds.

WARRIORS *of the* RAINBOW

When the Earth is sick and the animals have disappeared, there will come a tribe of people from all beliefs, colours and cultures who believe in actions, not words, and who will restore the Earth to its former beauty. This tribe will be called 'The Warriors of the Rainbow'.

ANCIENT AMERICAN INDIAN LEGEND

Planet Earth is 4,600,000,000 years old. If we condense this time span we can compare it to a person 46 years old. Only at the age of 42 did the Earth begin to flower. Dinosaurs and the great reptiles did not appear until one year ago, when the planet was 45. Mammals arrived only eight months ago and in the middle of last week, human-like apes developed into ape-like humans, and last weekend, the last ice age covered the Earth.

Modern man has been around for 4 hours. During the last hour agriculture was discovered. The Industrial Revolution began a minute ago. Since then, people have made a rubbish tip of Paradise. We have multiplied our numbers to plague proportions, caused the extinction of 500 species of animals, turned the planet upside-down in the search for fuels, and now we stand, like brutish infants, arrogant with power, on the edge of a war to end all wars, and close to effectively destroying this oasis of life in the solar system.

1   Find words in the texts which mean the following:
1   a group of people
2   give back/repair
3   put into a smaller space
4   a kind of monkey
5   a place where you put all the things you do not want
6   increased
7   a disease which gets out of control
8   ceasing to exist
9   extremely proud

2   Complete these sentences in your own words:
1   The American Indians believed _____.
2   In the text, the writer thinks that people have _____.
3   When the writer calls people *brutish infants* he is comparing us to _____.
4   In this unit we expect to hear/read more about _____.

3   Read the text about Planet Earth again, and look at the picture. Now discuss with a partner how it relates to the second text and which part in particular it summarises.

Greenpeace is an organisation which works to arouse people's interest in what is happening to the environment and life systems of our planet. It also asks questions and demands answers. It wants to know what is going to be done in terms of actions and laws to reverse the process of destruction. Few people did much to protest against the damage to the planet until Greenpeace was formed. If they did know what governments or companies were doing to damage the delicate balance of life in the sea, or on land, then they said little, or nothing at all. If they cared about what was happening, then they had no way of expressing it.

4   Refer to the box above to answer these questions.
1   Find a sentence in the text which tells you a particular question which Greenpeace is asking.
2   Find another which tells you about the purpose of Greenpeace.
3   Find a sentence which tells you what people did before Greenpeace was formed.
4   The text tells us that although people might have worried about what was happening there was no way for them to discuss the matter publicly. Which sentence tells us this?

5   Greenpeace wants to know what is going to be done. Match Columns **A** and **B** in order to find out some of the things the organisation is concerned about. Work in pairs and talk to your partner, like this:
I think Greenpeace wants to know what is going to be done about the destruction of _____.

A	B
the spread of	elephants
the killing of	nuclear weapons
the hunting of	the rainforests
the destruction of	whales
the testing of	acid rain
	seals

6 Work in pairs. In Column **A** below you will find a list of animals, people and places. In Column **B** you will find what happened to them, but not in the correct order. Find out what happened by asking and answering questions, like this:
Michael, do you know what happened to the dodo?
– Yes, I think it ____ .

A	B
The dodo The American Indians The forests of Great Britain The wolves in Western Europe The Indians of South America The dinosaurs The Maoris of New Zealand	were placed on special reservations. became extinct a few hundred years ago. are still living there. died out in most countries many years ago. were cut down many centuries ago. were badly affected by European diseases. became extinct millions of years ago.

Check with other people, like this:
What did you say happened to the dodo?
– We said that it ____ .

7 The tribe will be called 'The Warriors of the Rainbow'. Work in groups. Imagine you are responsible for arranging a huge conference to spread the ideas of an organisation which is concerned with saving the world's environment. First, decide on a name for your organisation. Now, look at the activities below. These activities take place between now and the date of the conference, which is in six months' time. Decide when each of these activities is going to take place, and exactly how long each activity lasts. Some of the activities may take place at the same time. Take notes as you discuss this.

opening ceremony held
brochures designed and distributed
letters sent to the press
hotels and accommodation arranged
interviews with the press organised
the conference hall booked
speakers invited

When you have finished talk to other groups, like this:
What is the name of your organisation?
When will your letters to the press be sent?
When will your advertising be placed in the media?

8 Now write five sentences comparing your schedule with those of other people, like this:
In our conference the ____ will be ____ in the month of ____/from ____ to ____ . However, in Peter's group it won't be done until ____ .

9 Listen to the following people speaking and note whether they agree or disagree with the statements.

	Juan	Maria
Dolphins and whales should not be kept in captivity.		
No one should hunt whales.		
It is stupid to explore space.		

Now listen again, and this time write down the agreement and disagreement statements that they make. Use these guides:
Interviewer: Do you feel it's a waste of time?
Maria: ____ , it's a ____ ____ ____ and ____ .
Juan: I ____ ____ ____ ____ , Maria. The human race . . .
Juan: . . . no animals should be kept in captivity. I ____ ____ ____ .
Juan: As for hunting whales at sea, well I think ____ ____ ____ that it's ____ . What do you think, Maria?
Maria: ____ .

10 Work in groups of four. Take it in turns to express the opinions below, and respond to the views of others, like this:
I think/I don't think ____ .
– So do I./Neither do I./I disagree with that.
Then give a reason to support your agreement, or disagreement, using these words:
The reason I feel that way is ____ .
This is because ____ .
1 I think that the world's population is too big.
2 I think that generally all people in the world eat too much.
3 My friend thinks that we shouldn't eat meat.
4 I don't like nuclear power.
5 I think that there should be more pollution controls.
6 I think that we shouldn't hunt whales.

GRAMMAR SUMMARY

***What* as subject (of an embedded question)**
Greenpeace wants to know what is going to be done.
Do you know what happened to the dodo?

Future passive
When will your letters to the press be sent?

"Animalspeak"

Some years ago, Roger Payne, a member of the New York Zoological Society, was walking along the beach when he came upon a small porpoise. It was stranded. And it had been mutilated. Someone had cut off its tail for a souvenir. Besides this, two other people had cut their initials deeply into its side, and someone else had stuck a cigar in its blowhole. 'I removed the cigar,' he said, 'and stood there for a long time with feelings I cannot describe.'

He decided then to learn about the whale family, so that he might be able to have some effect on its future.

Humpback whales became one of the main targets of the voracious international whaling industry at the turn of the century. Since then whaling has reduced the world population of whales by 95%. As a result of this, humpbacks are currently protected by International Whaling Commission regulations. This is

fortunate because Payne, and others like him, discovered that the humpback sings and it is now known worldwide for its beautiful underwater songs.

Perhaps we have been slow to recognise animal language because of the varied forms it takes: the grinding of teeth, rattling of tails or spines or feathers, stamping the feet or using the chest as a drum. Animals sing, call, whistle, tap, drum, chirp, roar and snap. More and more is being discovered about how animals talk to each other. Is it partly due to this that we are increasingly concerned about the protection of endangered species, and the humane treatment of animals?

1 Read the passage above and find another way of saying the following:
1 badly damaged by people
2 greedy
3 in the early 1900s
4 total number of whales
5 rules
6 animals becoming extinct

2 Say whether these statements are correct.
1 When Roger Payne saw the porpoise, he felt he couldn't describe what had happened.
2 There are one-twentieth as many whales now as there were in 1900.
3 People have been slow to discover animal language because there are so many animals.

Complete these sentences in your own words.
1 Roger Payne decided to learn about whales because ____.
2 Whales are now protected ____.
3 The writer thinks that because ____.

3 Some animals communicate by grinding their teeth. Column **A** below shows some of the sounds made by the animals in Column **B**. Some of them are quite surprising. Use your dictionary to match the columns, then compare answers, like this:
I think that some snakes rattle their tails. What do you think?

A	B
snakes	grind their teeth
peacocks	clap their beaks together
gorillas	rattle their spines
rabbits	whistle with their wings
porcupines	rattle their feathers
fish	rattle their tails
storks	use their chests as drums
mute swans	trill with high speed wings
hummingbirds	stamp their large hind feet

4 Peter Tyack, who recorded humpback whales with Roger Payne, is describing his experiences. Listen and decide in which order he describes the following.
1 What sometimes happens when they're alone in the boat.
2 How he feels about seeing a wild animal unexpectedly.
3 The way it feels to be in the water with a humpback whale.
4 What happened one day when he was alone.

Listen again and answer the questions below.
1 The speaker uses two words which mean *vibrate* or *shake*. What are they?
2 How often are they alone in the boat?
3 What are the three words he uses to describe his experiences?

Now complete these sentences:
1 He felt he was being watched when ____.
2 The whale was hopping and lifting its head because ____.

11

5 Peter Tyack says he was sitting in the boat when he felt he was being watched. Have you ever felt you were being watched by an animal (or a human being), or followed or talked about? Talk to your partner, like this:
Have you ever felt you were being watched? – Yes, I have. Once when I was taking the dog for a walk ____. Find out as much as you can about the situation from your partner and take notes. Then write a short description about your partner beginning *Taking his dog for a walk one night, Robert felt ____.*

Bats are out at night and at this time their vision is poor. The saying *as blind as a bat* is not true. Bats are not blind, but the way they live makes sight unnecessary. Some bats can fly in total darkness and to do this they use echolocation. They send out high frequency sounds which bounce off targets. The returning echo is received and understood by the bat, which has very specialised hearing. From this it can find its target.

6 Read the caption about bats. The saying *as blind as a bat* is used to describe people who cannot see very well or will not wear their glasses. People are often compared to animals, and the columns below give some incomplete expressions. First match the columns. Then decide with your partner what they mean and if they are true. Talk to each other like this:
I think there is an expression 'as blind as a bat,' but I don't think/don't know if bats are blind.

A	B
ox	wise
dog	gentle
mule	quiet
lamb	strong
lion	sly
owl	stubborn
snake	sick
pig	brave
fox	slow
mouse	busy
bee	slippery
tortoise	dirty

Do you have these expressions in your language? What other expressions do you have like these?

The crocodile has survived, little changed, for 200 million years. The female lays up to ninety eggs in a pit in the sand by the side of a lake or river. The nest pit is covered and guarded by the female, until the young are ready to emerge. At hatching time the young crocodiles call for the mother to come and release them from the nest. When they detect the mother's footsteps they begin to chirp, until she reaches the pit and digs them out.

Pigs communicate a lot. Piglets, for example, have a contact call that they make when a litter becomes separated. *Adults have warning barks for strangers and *greeting honks for familiar farm workers. *Pigs, it seems, make happy and unhappy sounds. A pig will protest if another lies on top of it. And *there is a call asking for food.
(*See Exercise 9.)

Frogs, it has been said, divide their world into three classes of objects: if it's small enough you eat it; if it's big you run away from it; and if it's intermediate you mate with it. In order that frogs mate with the right objects, they rely on sound to attract females. There are frogs and toads that chirp, others croak, some whistle, and there are those that click.

7 Read the descriptions above of the way some more animals use sounds. Then find the words which mean the following. The number tells you which text to refer to.
2 come out   let out   sense
3 get in touch with   show disapproval
4 medium-sized   depend on

8 Read the captions again and, in pairs, complete the chart as in the example.

animal	sound	reason
young crocodiles	calling chirp	hear their mother ready to hatch
litter of piglets		
pigs		
frogs		
bats		

Now make sentences like this, to explain when or why each animal uses sound:
Young crocodiles use a calling chirp when they hear their mother/to say they are ready to hatch.

9 Look at photograph 3. Rewrite the caption, replacing each asterisk (*) with one of these words or phrases: also in addition to this   besides (this) as well as (this)

10 Not everyone likes all animals all of the time. Tell your partner about five animals you dislike and why. Your partner takes notes. Then write a paragraph about your partner using the words and phrases given in Exercise 9.

GRAMMAR SUMMARY

Past continuous passive
Have you ever felt you were being watched?

Connectors
As well as this, there is a call asking for food.

To/In order to
Young crocodiles use a calling chirp to say they are ready to hatch.

11

THE *Living* DEPARTMENT STORE

You know what you like. Here's where you can find it.

For you

You know what you like. The problem is, where to find it (and how to afford it). And once you look good, how do you go about creating a setting to match: furniture and fabrics, crockery and cookware, food and drink. Because they all say something about you and how you feel.

For your family

Clothes for children which are both high quality and top fashion are often hard to find. And children like to look good too. Not just teenagers, but from a very young age children are fashion conscious. They like to be up to date and comfortable. And the way they look can affect the way they act and feel.

Our shops offer clothes for all ages, and a world of good design. You will like our definition of good design too: we think there ought to be high quality at reasonable prices, whether you are just starting out or are coming up in the world.

12

---

1 Read the texts above and find words which mean:
have enough money for something   begin
making   aware   modern   influence

Now answer these questions:
1 How does the text make the reader feel good?
2 What does it say about the importance of clothes which suit the individual?
3 Where in the text is money mentioned?

2 Look at the illustrations above and find an example of the following:
trainers dufflecoat windcheater settee
spotlight holdall oven glove wellingtons
carrycot cubes glassware swing bin

Now ask and answer in pairs, like this:
What are trainers?   – I think they're a kind of _____.
Compare your answers with other pairs, like this:
Where are the trainers?   – They're in the first/ second/picture, next to/on the right of/ beside _____ etc.

3 Find the Living Department Store's description of good design. In small groups describe the following in a similar way: a good family car   a good education   a good boss   a good job   a good leisure activity.
Now compare your definitions with other groups.

4 Work in pairs, **A** and **B**. Listen to Edmund Barclay talking about his theory of design and take notes about the topics in either **A** or **B** below.

A	B
good design/designer	the consumer
the public	a definition of good design
natural fibres	beautiful things
personal taste	an antique collector

Talk in pairs about what he said, like this:
What did he say about good design and the designer?   – He said that good design was a designer's duty.

5 Listen to the tape again and find expressions which mean the same as the words in italic below.
What is your *general approach?*
I *very strongly believe* that good design is a duty.
A lot of people *take* less because they *don't have enough money.*
Isn't good design *a question* of taste?
When we talk about individual taste, *a very important word* is 'appropriate'.
Is the product *correct for this* particular person?

Use the words from the tape to complete these sentences:
1 I don't think she ought to _____ those damaged goods.
2 I _____ that this is the best design for you.
3 _____ habits _____, _____ 'unpredictable'.
4 Taste is often _____ of what you can _____.
5 _____ dress _____ a person who is overweight?

Anna Wood shops at the Living Department Store. She describes herself as a typical mother of two children (aged nine and ten), with a professional job, and a home and family to buy for. She is looking for value for money. Previously she shopped all over London. Now time, and money, quite often bring her to a store like this one. For example, she used to buy her children's clothes in three or four shops in central London. Now she buys them all here.

6   In pairs build up a pattern of Anna Wood's previous shopping habits by completing the table below. Ask and answer questions like this: *Where did she use to buy _____?*
Compare with other pairs, like this:
What did you say about _____?   – We said that she used to buy _____ in a _____.

	supermarket	department store	local shop	superstore	*specialist shop
kitchen furniture					
kitchen equipment					
sports clothes					
child's trainers					
living room furniture					
nappies and toys					
garden equipment					
curtains					
her casual clothing					
her formal clothing					
her husband's shirts					
her husband's jackets					

*For example: hardware store, children's shop, sports shop, furniture store, ladies' shop, men's shop, garden centre, shoe shop, baby shop

7   How have your buying habits changed? Write where you used to buy the items below and where you buy them now. What brands did you use to buy? Do you still buy the same ones? Make notes, like this:
– used to buy Yves St Laurent clothes/Harrods
– now buy . . .

Items: clothes, furniture, frozen food, toiletries, shoes

Talk to your partner like this:
Where did you use to buy your _____? – I used to buy them at _____ but now I prefer _____.
What kind of _____ do you buy? – I usually buy the ones sold/made by _____ because they are more/less expensive (last longer, look better etc.)

> A design empire is just one example of many types of things being sold or designed by one company or group. The small specialist shop is threatened by large chains who can sell things more cheaply, and all under one roof.

8   Below is a list of things which may be sold in specialist shops in the UK, but can now be found in many other places. Match the items in Column **A** with the shops in Column **B**.

A	B
football	off licence
toothbrush	chemist's
wine	newsagent's
strawberries	hardware store
envelopes	electrical shop
magazines	book shop
wedding ring	greengrocer's
light bulb	confectioner's
cough medicine	dairy
dictionary	fruiterer's
chocolate	jeweller's
eggs	sports shop

Now ask and answer in pairs, like this:
Where were cosmetics sold ten years ago in the UK?   – I'm not sure but I think it/they used to be sold in/bought from a _____.
What about in (name of country)?   – It/they used to be _____, but now you can buy it/them in a _____ (department store, superstore, supermarket).

9   Look at the pair of photographs below, showing two very different types of rooms. Which room (or items) do you prefer, and why? Tell your partner like this:
I like the room at the top best/better than the room at the bottom because it is more modern. I think the furniture is nicer and more comfortable etc.

Now change partners and report what your old partner said, like this:
She said she liked that room better because it's more modern.

12

10   Choose one of the following roles: An Italian artist/craftsman (makes jewellery); a leading French fashion designer; a fashion reporter; a teenager; a director of a design empire.
Write one reason why you think a huge design empire might be a good thing, and one reason why it might be a bad thing. Report back to the class and discuss. Then write up a short summary of one or two of the different views.

GRAMMAR SUMMARY

Prepositions
They're next to/on the right of . . .

***Used to*/past simple**
Where did she buy . . .?
She used to buy . . .

Comparison
I think the furniture is more comfortable.

OPTING OUT

'I want my children to learn values which are different from the values of the modern industrial world. These values are generally bad.'

These are the words of a man of 39, living in south-west England. Seventeen years ago, when he left university, he was going to be an engineer. He had a degree, was highly trained, and had ambitions. However, after working for only six months in London, he left his job and went out into the country.

Today, he lives in a stonebuilt house just outside a village. A small piece of land at the back of the house produces vegetables – beans, peas, cabbages, potatoes and lettuce. There are also chickens, running free through the garden. The house is clean, well kept. As you walk through the rooms you see nothing that isn't necessary. There are a great number of books; on the other hand there aren't any ornaments. They have electric light, but no television, and no radio. Wood is used in the fireplaces. The rooms are all spotless, bright and tidy.

You do not expect to see children. Nevertheless, there are five of them, ranging in age from twelve down to two. Gerald's wife, Judy, is in the kitchen, which again is bright and clean. It's not long, as you look around, before you notice that once again there are certain differences between this house and most others. There are no tins of food, for example, and the flour, sugar and salt come in barrels, not bags. If you look closely, you can see that while the cooker is electric, there are no other electrical appliances at all, except for a very old fridge. No washing machine. No dishwasher. No food processor. But open a cupboard, and you find rows of bottled jams, and fruit. Open another and you come across a sack of rice, and another a sack of beans.

1 Read the text and say if the following are true or false.
1 The text says what Gerald was going to be after he left university.
2 It tells you how long he worked.
3 The text says Gerald met his wife in London.
4 The text says how many children there are.
5 Gerald was 20 when he left university.
6 The text tells you when he got married.

2 What do these words in the text describe? For example: *highly trained* describes Gerald
bad   highly trained   stonebuilt
well kept   bright   old   bottled

Find things in the text which the writer considers unnecessary.
There are two words in the text which mean *but*. What are they?

3 Obviously we haven't heard everything about Gerald. In groups, decide on one more thing you wouldn't be surprised to find out. This might be a fact – like the lack of a washing machine – or an attitude which you think he might have.
Decide on which of these adjectives would describe your feelings best, if you were Judy (add other words, if you like):
content   discontent   worried   angry
proud   happy

Discuss your ideas with other groups.

4 Below is a family of six people. Choose a job for each of them from the list below, then ask and answer questions, like this:
Do you know what Judith and Michael are doing now?   – Yes, I do. Judith is a _____, while Michael has become a _____.

People: Judith, Michael, Kate, Gordon, Bill, Maureen
Jobs: computer programmer, lorry driver, nurse, engineer, gardener, photographer

Four of these people changed their minds about jobs when they finished training. Decide which ones changed their minds, and choose what they were going to be from the following list: Then talk about the people, like this:
Judith was going to be a _____.
– Why did she change her mind?
Because (of) _____.

surgeon, airline pilot, company director, social worker

5 Think about things you/your parents (or members of your family) were going to do at some time in your lives, but didn't. Ask and answer questions in pairs, like this:
Is there anything you were going to do in the past, but didn't do?
– Yes, I (my mother/father/brother etc.) was going to become a _____/was going to visit _____/work in _____, but I/he/she didn't.
Oh, and why was that?
– Because _____.

Report to others about what people say, like this:
Rolf said that his father was going to become a doctor but he didn't because _____.

13

6 In the text we see that Gerald and Judy can enjoy the quiet of the country. On the other hand, there are things they can't enjoy or do, like going to the cinema. Think of your own lives, and ask and answer questions, like this:
What are some of the things you can do where you live? – Well, I can go swimming/ fishing/take a walk in the ____/go to the ____. On the other hand, I can't ____.

7 In groups of three or four build up a list of things which you really like about the place in which you live. Also build up a list of things you don't like. You might decide on things such as parks, open spaces, busy shops, entertainment, cinemas, tourists, international atmosphere etc.

Now report to the rest of the class, like this:
Michael said he likes the clean air. However, he doesn't like the ____.

Write summaries about the people in your group/class, like this:
Christine likes the ____, while Dagmar likes the ____. Peter likes the ____ and the ____. However, he doesn't like the ____.

8 Listen to Gerald's wife. We spoke to her when her husband was out. Then answer these questions:
1 Judy says that they are like millions of other people. What does she mean?
2 The interviewer says something about Gerald to show that he is different. What exactly does he say?
3 The interviewer's comment is not finished, however. How would you finish it?
4 What bad habits do you think Judy is talking about?
5 Is Judy happy with her lifestyle?

9 Look at this sentence from the listening text:
Judy says she gets her money tomorrow.
Why does she use the present simple tense about 'tomorrow'?

Here is a timetable for a course you have booked, on self-sufficiency. You are discussing it with a friend, who is also coming on the course. Part of the timetable is fixed, and part is optional. Complete your timetable by talking to your friend, like this:
On Tuesday afternoon I have basic cookery. What do you have?
– I've got ____. Where is the problems class on Monday morning?

10 In groups, decide on how much you agree with what Gerald and his wife have done. Agree on one or two statements which you think summarise the situation best. Now compare these statements with other groups.

Here are some typical situations which some people call opting out. First, say why some people think they are opting out. Then give your opinion. Do you agree with them or not? Discuss what you think the lifestyles of these people may be.

Hermit

Hippy

Buddhist monk

Choose one of the above, and write two paragraphs: one describing the lifestyle, another giving your opinion.

This week-long course is intended to help you plan your venture into self-sufficiency. The morning lectures are all obligatory, the afternoon ones are options which you choose.

SCHEDULE

	a.m.	p.m.
Monday		*or* Vegetable gardening (Room 7)
Tuesday	(Room 2) Bookkeeping (Room)	Basic cookery (Room 6) *or*
Wednesday	(Room)	*or* Principles of preserving food (Room 8)
Thursday	Basics of crop farming (Room 2)	Selling your produce (Room 6) *or*
Friday	(Room 4)	*or* Co-operative farming (Room 7)

SCHEDULE

	a.m.	p.m.
Monday	Problems of self-sufficiency (Room)	Small livestock (Room 6) *or*
Tuesday	(Room 3)	*or* Principles of freezing food (Room 8)
Wednesday	Handling your Bank Manager (Room 2)	Milk & cheese products (Room 6) *or*
Thursday	(Room)	*or* Large livestock (Room 7)
Friday	Basics of live-stock farming (Room)	Herbal medicine (Room 8) *or*

This weeklong course is intended to help you plan your venture into self-sufficiency. The morning lectures are all obligatory, the afternoon ones are options which you choose.

13

FESTIVALS OF LIGHT

Swedish travel correspondent, Berit Andersson, has recently returned from the Far East. While visiting India and Thailand she had the opportunity of being present at two exotic festivals: Diwali in India, and Loy Kratong in Thailand. Here, she writes of her experiences.

For millions of Hindus, New Year comes in October or November, and it is marked by perhaps the gayest of all Indian Festivals — Diwali. I was lucky to be there this year, travelling from Delhi to Calcutta by train after a wonderful period of two weeks in the Himalayas. When I arrived I was surprised at the size of the crowds in the streets — many more people than I had expected. But besides that, there was an enormous amount of noise, and sudden flashes of light in the night sky. My friends in Calcutta told me that on this night every city, town and village is turned into a fairyland, with thousands of flickering oil lamps and electric lights illuminating homes and public places. As well as the lights on the ground, the sky was full of the noise and flashes of thousands of fire-crackers and fire missiles, which seemed to rush endlessly up from the ground.

That night was so different from the evening I spent on the banks of the river Ping in the North of Thailand just a few weeks later. I was with some friends just on the outskirts of the beautiful city of Chiengmai, watching the dark river looking so silently alive under the thousands of tiny lights floating on its surface.

This was the night of Loy Kratong, a festival whose purpose is to give thanks to the 'Mother of Water'. A *kratong* is a special construction, which can be simply of paper or banana leaves, and which is floated on the rivers, canals and lakes of the country on the night of the full moon in the month of November. Some *kratongs* are much more complex and consist of thousands of small flowers. In addition, each *kratong* carries a candle, and sometimes a stick of incense and a coin. The candle is lit, and the *kratong* floated gently into the stream — and if the *kratong* floats until the candle has burnt out, tradition says that your wishes will be granted.

---

1 Read the text and say if the following are true or false.
1 The report was probably written in India.
2 One of the festivals is quieter than the other.
3 The new year is not always marked by 1st January.
4 A Thai would prefer the candle to go out quickly.
5 The writer went straight to Delhi after arriving in India.

2 Answer these questions, firstly with reference to Diwali and then to Loy Kratong.
1 What was the purpose of the festival?
2 What time of year does it take place?
3 What can be seen in the air?
4 What can be seen on the ground/water?

3 Answer the following questions about the text.
1 Berit says the sky was 'full of noise'. Why was this?
2 Why does Berit say the water was 'silently alive'?
3 Berit says the river was dark. On a night with no clouds, do you think the night of Loy Kratong would also be very dark?
4 Berit mentions the great difference between the two festivals. What was she thinking of?

4 While visiting India and Thailand, Berit Andersson had the opportunity of seeing some festivals. Using the list of festivals in the box, ask and answer in pairs about two travellers, Jay and Anna, like this:
Did Jay see anything special while staying in/ travelling around/visiting Thailand?

— Yes, while staying in Thailand, he saw the festival of _____.
Oh, and where was that?
— It was in _____.
Did he see anything else while staying there?

Anna/India		Jay/Thailand	
festival	*place*	*festival*	*place*
Onam	Kerala	Loy Kratong	Phuket
Holi	Mathura	Songkran	Chiengmai
Diwali	Calcutta	Rocket Festival	Yasothon

14

5 Now listen to the tape. You will hear Jay and Anna talking about some of the festivals they visited. As you listen, make notes in a chart, like the one below.

	Time of year	Celebrates	Activities
Onam			
Holi			
Songkran			
Rocket Festival			

6 Using the information in the text, and from the tape (see answers to Exercise 5 above) ask and answer questions, like this:
What was Anna doing during the first part of November? — She was in the town of ____, India, watching ____ (name of festival).

7 When visiting India, Berit gave a radio interview about festivals in the West, and especially in her native Sweden. Listen to an extract from the interview where she is talking about the festival of Lucia. You will hear these expressions used: *besides her/as well as this/in addition.* Listen and answer these questions:
1 What does *her* in the expression *besides her* refer to?
2 What does *this* in the expression *as well as this* refer to?
3 When the expression *in addition* is used, what does Berit tell us they had to drink?
4 When the interviewer says that the sight must be fantastic, does Berit agree or not? What does she say it looks like?
5 Berit gives an example of the festival from her childhood. Listen for what she says and complete this sentence: *I remember ____ in the morning.*

14

Diwali (India)	a lot of lights everywhere	a lot of fire-crackers
Guy Fawkes (UK)	a lot of fireworks	a bonfire
Midsummer (Sweden)	many decorations of flowers	dancing in the day and evening
Festival of Flowers (Thailand)	parades of flowered floats	displays of exotic plants
Pooram (India)	spectacular parades of elephants	firework displays
Edinburgh (UK)	first class musical events	very good theatre

8 The chart above gives information about other festivals around the world. Work in pairs, and ask and answer, using these phrases: in addition to (this)   besides (that)   as well as (this)
What can you tell me about Diwali? — There are a lot of lights everywhere. Besides that there are also a lot of fire-crackers.

9 Berit remembers waking early in the morning. Think of a holiday or festival you have been to, and ask and answer questions in pairs, like this:

Can you tell me any festivals/holidays you remember well?
— Yes, I remember ____.
Is there anything you can remember doing?
— Yes, I remember ____ing ____.

10 You wish to get a list of festivals in India or Thailand, and you write to the Thai or Indian Embassy in your country, asking for details. Write a letter, explaining when and where you are going, and asking for their help.

11 In groups, plan an itinerary for some friends who are visiting your country. Include visits to festivals and fairs which will be taking place. When you have finished, compare your itinerary with those of other groups, using *besides, in addition, as well as,* like this:
What have you planned? — Well, we've decided that they should visit ____, but besides that, they are also going to visit ____.

GRAMMAR SUMMARY

While + -ing
While staying in Thailand, Jay saw the festival of ____.

Remember + -ing
I remember waking up in the morning.

***Besides, as well as, in addition* (to)**
There are lots of lights everywhere. Besides that, there are also fire-crackers.

A HOLIDAY WITH A DIFFERENCE

Holiday resorts may not be your cup of tea. But that is no reason for avoiding Tunisia. Look at these ancient sites of Tunisia – as exciting as any in the world, and including a colosseum to rival the one in Rome. So why not join a professional archaeologist for a seven-day holiday with a difference – a guided tour of the magnificent ruins of Carthaginian and Roman Tunisia.

1 Read the text and say whether these statements are true or false.
1 You can't drink tea in Tunisia.
2 Tunisia hasn't got any holiday resorts.
3 The colosseum in Tunisia is better than the one in Rome.
4 This tour is for professional archaeologists.
5 The Romans took over from the Carthaginians in Tunisia.

15

Carthage is the ruin most often visited by tourists. It was founded some time before 800 BC by Phoenicians from the Eastern Mediterranean. After the Romans completely destroyed Carthage in 146 BC, Julius Caesar rebuilt it in 46 BC, when it grew to a huge size before being destroyed again by Arab invaders. It has been difficult to excavate Carthage because it was so thoroughly destroyed by the Romans. Still, there is a great deal to see, including the wonderful view over the Gulf to Tunis, and a little thought and imagination will bring the bare bones back to life.

Hammamet is a lovely garden resort, in which no hotel may be built higher than the tallest local tree. Not only is there a lovely curving beach of fine, silver sand, but sunbathing is equally enjoyable in the grounds of the luxury hotels with their palm trees, exotic flowers and multi-coloured birdlife. Visit the picturesque fifteenth century medina (old town) and kasbah, from which many wonderful souvenirs, blankets, leather and embroidered goods can be bought. Or stroll along the beach in the early evening and look at the brightly-painted fishing boats.

Kerkouane is a truly amazing Carthaginian archaeological site. It is quite easily reached on foot along the beach from Mansoura. When it was first discovered in 1952, there was great excitement about the streets and house plans uncovered. At first no public buildings were found, and one rather silly theory was that it had been a holiday resort in the fifth century BC. Almost all the houses are the same, with a small courtyard, a well and an altar. They are most famous, however, for their baths, neatly lined with reddish cement, and every house has its own. The town was abandoned some time in the second century BC, after the destruction of Carthage, and never reoccupied by the Romans, which is why it is so well preserved.

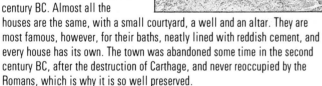

South to El Djem for a sight that will take your breath away. The extraordinary amphitheatre at El Djem is the single most impressive Roman monument in Africa. It is even more magnificent because of its sudden appearance, in the middle of a flat plain, surrounded by a huddle of small houses. What is still left of the amphitheatre is one of the best preserved of its kind, finer than the Colosseum in Rome, and not a great deal smaller.

2 Read the captions by the photographs and complete the chart below. In some cases there will be more than one town.

Kelibia is a fishing port and still remains the most peaceful resort in the country. It has a romantic castle ruin and hotels to which many people go just to enjoy their superb grilled fresh sardines.

	name of town/s
1 Was this an ancient holiday resort?	
2 This town was destroyed by the Romans.	
3 Archaeologists were amazed to find baths in individual houses here.	
4 Good place for fresh fish.	
5 Carthaginian site.	
6 There are ruins here.	
7 It is often compared with Rome.	
8 Somewhere to go for peace and quiet.	
9 Many gladiators died here.	
10 Holiday resort famous for its beach, flowers and palms.	

3   Listen to the tape and complete the itinerary below.

Day one	Arrive _____. Coach to La Marsa. _____ and free time to _____.
Day two	An early start to see _____. Breakfast and lecture followed by coach journey to see _____ of Mansoura. Lunch provided from the best of the fishermen's catch. Four hour combined walk and lecture to Kerkouane (_____ also available), one of the most _____. Coach to Kelibia in time for _____.
Day three	Coach to Hammamet – free day to enjoy this _____
Day four	Coach to the ruin of El Djem, a _____. Have lunch in Sfax and _____ to beautiful Kerkenna Islands.
Day five	
Day six	Coach to Great Mosque of Kairouan. Picnic lunch. Coach to Bizerte.
Day seven	_____ Utica. Lunch. Coach to Tunis international airport. Depart.

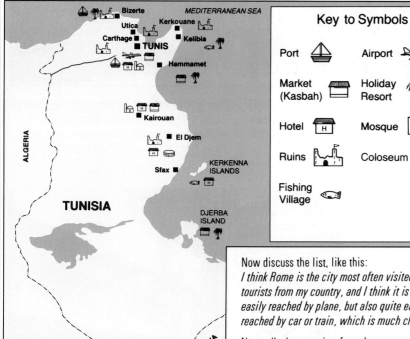

Key to Symbols

Port · Airport · Market (Kasbah) · Holiday Resort · Hotel · Mosque · Ruins · Coloseum · Fishing Village

7   Listen to the tape and answer the questions below. A Tunisian guide is describing a Roman circus like the ones held at El Djem.
1   What was the purpose of the Roman Circus? Which words tell you?
2   Why were there royal boxes at both ends of the arena?
3   What wasn't always given to the defeated gladiator?
4   What signs did the crowd and/or the official give the defeated gladiator?
5   Name three ways that the shows became more brutal.
6   What was the most worrying thing about the shows?

8   *Roman rulers gave their subjects circus shows to keep them happy.* Tour operators are often worried about the special needs of their clients, and they must find out from hotels what special arrangements they will make.
You and your partner manage a large hotel. Together, fill in the chart below, saying what special things you do for parents, older people, children etc. Then another pair interviews you, like this:
What do you give to/do for children? — We give them/they are given a special menu.

category of guests	special arrangements
Older people	
Newly married couples	
Sports enthusiasts	
Teenagers	
Children under twelve	
Babies	
Parents of small children	

Now discuss the list, like this:
I think Rome is the city most often visited by tourists from my country, and I think it is most easily reached by plane, but also quite easily reached by car or train, which is much cheaper.

Now talk about tourists from these countries:
USA   UK   Japan

4   *Carthage is the ruin most often visited by tourists.* Look at the list below of cities and countries which are popular with tourists and add some other places popular with people in your own country. Then discuss in pairs the places visited by tourists from your country and how to get to them, as in the example below.

Rome Morocco Tunisia Yugoslavia
Hamburg UK USA Japan Spain Mexico
Brazil Australia

5   In groups ask and answer questions about your own towns, like this:
Which places are quite (very/most) easily reached on foot (by bus/by car/metro/train etc.)? Which places are quite/very frequently crowded/empty?

6   Look at the map and the photographs and make sentences from the table below to write notes about the map, like this:
Tunis is a port from which you can go to Genoa.

Tunis El Djem Djerba A kasbah Utica Hammamet Bizerte Kelibia Kerkenna	is has	port town island market place airport hotel	for from on in at	which	you can go to Genoa. there is a famous Colosseum. there is a holiday resort. you can buy souvenirs and leather. you can find ruins. you can find fishing boats. you can stay overnight.

9   You are at the end of your holiday in Tunisia and you want to take presents back to your family and friends. Make a list of the people you want to buy presents for and discuss it with your partner, like this:
I want to buy something for my mother. — How old is she?/Does she like _____?/Has she ever been given _____?

GRAMMAR SUMMARY

Deleted relative (in the passive)
Carthage is the ruin most often visited by tourists.

Relative *which* + preposition
Tunis is a port from which you can go to Genoa.

15

⬤ ART AT THE CENTRE

The Pompidou Centre
– Anyone can enter

Art amateurs, book lovers, cinema lovers, anyone can enter and use this enormous cultural centre. Everyone can flip through the mass of newspapers, journals and books, listen to the latest releases in music, watch a special programme on television, have a drink or a cup of coffee. And everyone is free to talk to a neighbour or remain quiet and absorbed. It is quite a change from the traditional operation of libraries and museums.

The 'Beaubourg' was the dream of President Georges Pompidou, who died in 1974, three years before it was completed. It was built on the site of a car park in the Beaubourg district, a hub (or centre) of transportation in the middle of Paris. An international architectural competition was held in 1971, and 681 projects were submitted. The winning design was by a team of architects – Renzo Piano (Italy) and Richard Rogers (UK).

The Barbican Centre
– Home of the Royal Shakespeare Company

Opened in March 1982, the Barbican Centre is the home both of the Royal Shakespeare Company, one of the greatest theatre companies in the world, and the London Symphony Orchestra. It adjoins the famous Guildhall School of Music and Drama. The Centre is largely a centre for the performing arts, rather than the plastic arts and houses three cinemas, a concert hall, a main theatre and a studio theatre.

The Barbican is situated in a historical part of London, now the financial district, just outside the line of the wall which encircled the City in Roman times. A 'barbican' is a watchtower or gateway forming part of the outer defence of a city or castle. During the nineteenth and early twentieth centuries the area was the centre of the London textile and clothing industry. On 29th December 1940 a very large part of the area was devastated by bombing. In 1956 the Minister of Housing and Local Government proposed a residential district with schools, shops, open spaces and some kind of cultural centre.

1   Read about the Pompidou Centre and answer these questions:
1   What is it?   2   Where is it and why?
3   When was it built?
4   Why is it called the Pompidou Centre?
5   Why wasn't it built by French architects?
Read about the Barbican and answer these questions:
1   What is it?   2   Where is it and why?
3   Why is it called the Barbican?
Complete the following sentences:
1   Some examples of performing arts are ____.
2   ____ are examples of plastic arts.
3   The sort of people who visit the Pompidou Centre/Barbican are those who ____.
4   A traditional library or museum is ____.

2   Listen to the short dialogue and complete the questions below. Listen again and decide what function each question has. Is it asking for information, making a suggestion or demanding something?
1   Isn't the LSO ____?
2   Wouldn't you ____?
3   Won't you ____?
4   Couldn't you ____?

Listen to the seven sentences on the tape. What do you think each person is trying to do? Is he/she asking for information, making a suggestion or recommendation, or demanding something?

3   Write down the names of the following (from your town/country): cinema, nightclub, theatre, concert hall, sportsground/stadium. Write what/who is appearing at each one next Friday. Show your list to your partner and ask and answer like this, using *isn't/aren't, won't, wouldn't*:
Isn't André Previn appearing at the Barbican on Friday?   – Yes, he is.
Wouldn't you like to/Won't you come with me?   – Yes, I'd love to/Aren't Rangers playing at home on Friday? I'd rather not miss that game.

What's so special about the Beaubourg?

The Beaubourg was to be the first cultural institution in France devoted entirely to modern art, and to the new mass culture. The architects had a very definite idea of what the centre should be able to do: it must be able to integrate with the outside world and the surrounding district. It has to have a flexible structure, because it should be able to give a service to a large and changing public, for a hundred years or more. It must be able to provide general information about and exposure to modern art to an indiscriminate public. It is not only a place for displaying art, but somewhere that artists should be able to meet the public. Art is not only something to look at, but something to participate in.

The most important thing was that the centre must be able to help individuals understand modern art and culture. The centre is multi-purpose: it is a museum, but it is also a public library, an industrial age design centre and a music research centre. Those who use the Centre should not be just scholars and experts, but the general public.

4　Find words in the text above which mean the following:
blend/fit in with　　capable of change
without a lot of knowledge or judgement
join in actively with
Say whether or not the following statements are correct:
1　You are unlikely to find a seventeenth-century painting in the Pompidou Centre.
2　Art should be for artists, scholars, experts and the general public.
3　The purpose of the Centre is to educate people about modern art and culture.

5　Read the text again and find out what the architects thought the centre should/must be able to do. Make lists under the headings *should* and *must*. Then complete the words below and make sentences, saying what you think people should/must be able to see/do at a good arts centre, like this:
People should be able to see exhibitions of modern sculpture.
scu _ _ _ _ re　c _ _ ema　d _ _ ign　mu _ _ c
c _ _ fts　th _ _ _ re　l _ _ era _ _ _ _
pai _ _ _ ng　dan _ _ _ g

6　Write a paragraph about what people must/should be able to do in three of the following places and compare your answers with other people in the class.
a sports centre　hospital　school　church
office block　theatre
Talk to each other, like this:
I think people in a hospital should be able to have visitors at any time.　— I don't agree. I think they must be able to rest.

7　Listen to the description on the tape of why the Pompidou Centre is so special and answer the questions:
1　What does the word *controversial* mean?
2　Name the colours used in the Centre. What are they used for? Why are they used?
3　What words are used to describe the carnival square?
4　What does the escalator look like?
5　How is the view from the top described?
Now listen to the tape again and complete the text above and below the photographs.

**The building of the Centre _____
Without it _____.**

The centre is not a closed museum, _____. It is _____ with all its organs and systems outside, including the skeleton.

The centre has been built so that it can be changed completely inside: _____

_____ is outside the main structure and _____.

One of the unique features of the Piano-Rogers design is _____.

Anyone can find it

'Centre Beaubourg' or simply 'Beaubourg' is all you need to say to any Parisian, and you will be directed to Centre Georges Pompidou. It is located in central Paris and its colourful exterior is easy to see. The architects were concerned with a larger area than the building itself from the very beginning. They fought for a series of open spaces for pedestrians, so that they could see and approach the Centre from various directions and viewpoints. The surrounding area has been made into a large pedestrian district, with the traditional pleasures of the promenade and the sidewalk cafe.

Can anyone find it?

The Barbican Centre is located in the City of London, the financial district, east of the main city centre. The building is approached over various highwalks surrounded by high-rise office blocks and can be reached by bus or tube. There is no clear view of the building from any angle, and it is surrounded by The Barbican, which is a large development of private flats. When the centre first opened there were many jokes about 'getting lost in the Barbican' and now yellow lines lead pedestrians to its entrances from three different Underground stations.

8　Read the information about the location of the two centres. Then take notes under these headings about the Barbican and the Pompidou Centre, taking your information from the passages above and from the rest of the unit. Then, in groups, decide which arts centre you prefer and why. Use the following expressions: *must/should be able to, makes you want to _____.*
1　**Location** (where it is)
2　**View of exterior** (what it looks like)
3　**Approach/accessibility** (how easy it is to get there)
4　**Audience** (who it's for)
5　**Purpose** (what it's for)
6　**Facilities** (what it's got)

9　Write a short paragraph explaining how the Pompidou Centre and the Barbican are different. Compare the overall design, purpose, appearance, location, etc.

16

GRAMMAR SUMMARY

Negative questions
Isn't the LSO playing at the Barbican on Friday night?

Should/must be able to
People should be able to see exhibitions of modern sculpture.

SCENES FROM GREECE

Takis, a Greek photographer, is being interviewed about his art.

These postcards (and others a bit like them) are now a familiar sight in Greece. But until a few years ago, postcards of Greece were like postcards anywhere – beach scenes and small villages, olive groves and ruins, a windmill or a donkey. The man responsible for this change is Panagiotis Perrakis (Takis), a man who loves photography, and is obviously a master of his art. 'Ever since I first had a camera in my hand I have taken pictures,' he says. 'At first they were very bad pictures – all in black and white and either too dark or too light. I had a very good camera then – a Leica. It was given to my father, actually, and I used it all the time.' Since then he has studied photography in New York, London, then Germany. He ran a bookshop in Athens before

he started this business. Then, seven years ago, he started producing postcards.

Why postcards? I asked him. 'I am always being asked that,' he told me. 'It was not exactly my idea. A friend of mine gave me the idea. He thought I had spent enough money on cameras, and he thought that I should get something out of it. And I liked the idea. I didn't know what to do, and then I thought "I'll make some postcards". And I decided to do something different. It wouldn't have been very clever of me to make normal postcards like the others. So I tried something new. I don't know where the ideas come from. I try to put on paper some scenes from everyday life, some thoughts from my head, or some parts of books or poems I have read, and liked.'

1 Read the text and complete these sentences.
1 Postcards of Greece used to be ____.
2 This has changed because of ____, who ____.
3 Before he began to produce postcards seven years ago, he ____.
4 He chose postcards because ____.
5 His postcards were different because ____.

2 The text above is the result of an interview. What do you think Takis is being asked by the interviewer? Complete the questions below and then check with your partner, like this:
I think he's being asked when he became interested in photography? – I agree. I also think he's being asked if he ____.
1 When did you first ____?
2 What camera ____?

3 Have you ever ____?/Where ____?
4 What did you ____?
5 When did you ____?
6 Whose ____?
7 Where do the ____?

3 Takis says he is always being asked why he chose postcards. Here are some other occupations. What questions do you think they are always being asked? Make sentences as in the example.
Doctors: *I think they're always being asked how they feel when someone is very ill or dying.*
factory workers security guards
teachers police officers divers pilots
politicians lorry drivers
psychiatric nurses miners

4 Takis is describing the postcard with the old man (above left). Listen to the tape and find out what he says the Greeks have for breakfast and what the old man was thinking. These incomplete words all refer to photography. Listen to the tape again and complete them.
fi__ l__s f_l__r ca__ra
fo_u_es __t of f___s __ f_c__

5 *The old man didn't know he was being photographed.* In groups decide where each of you is being photographed and think of incomplete clue words, like this: __nny, Me____rr_n___, i_l__d, b__ch, (sunny, Mediterranean, island, beach,) Then give the words to other groups to complete and to try to guess where you are being photographed, by asking:
Are you being photographed on a Greek island? Are you windsurfing?

6 Takis has described four of the postcards on these pages and how they were taken. Here are some sentences from the descriptions. Which postcards do you think are being described?

I saw it but I passed by. Seconds later I realised I wanted it. Would she still be there?

I felt something in my throat like I had to swallow something and I couldn't, . . . the people who made that sign were in love.

Behind the musicians there was a mirror. There were too many reflections in that mirror, so I used a filter.

This gate is so beautiful. I had to do something special, something like a painting, for example.

Now listen to Takis describing the postcards on tape. Were you right?

7 Look at Takis' description below postcard *4*. It is incomplete. In pairs, decide which words should go in the blanks. Then listen to Takis on the tape. Were you right?

4

This is a scene from a Greek island and ____ this island everything is white. When I think of the sea, I ____ think of something white as well. ____ walls, for example, or white birds, white foam on the ____. Blue cannot just ____ plain blue. There ____ be something white. So I took a picture with just ____ walls and nothing else, and just the ____ railing there. And a bit of light blue ____.

8 Listen to the first part of the tape again and take notes. In pairs, write captions for each of the postcards. Compare your captions with other pairs, like this:
We've called the second postcard 'cat in jail' because/as/since ____.

5

A	B
He makes postcards	due to the number of reflections in the mirror
He used a filter	because the gate was so beautiful
He wanted to photograph the cat	because of the white houses and blue sky
He wanted to make it look like a painting	because of his love of photography
He wondered if he was jealous	as she looked like she was in jail
He took the photo on that island	since they seemed to be in love
The cat looked like she was in jail	because of the bars on the window
Greek postcards have changed	as a result of Takis' style of postcard

9 Takis says: *Since there were too many reflections, . . . I used a filter.* Here are some more words which show why: *due to/because of/as a result of/because/as*. Match the statements in Column **A** above with the reasons in Column **B** to write sentences, like this:
Greek postcards have changed as a result of Takis' style of postcard.

10 Match Columns **A** and **B** below to say why the people do what they do. Then talk to your partner, like this:
I think he became a ____ due to/as a result of his ____./I think she's a ____ because/since as ____. What do you think? – Yes, I agree with you./No, I think ____.

A	B
mime artist	likes colour
director	enjoys working alone
oil painter	love of Bach
photographer	loves entertaining people
comedian	has a sense of humour
sculptor	love of comedy
classical pianist	hatred of bad films
pop guitarist	likes working with images
concert flautist	likes playing with a large orchestra

6

11 Choose the postcard you like the most/least and give several reasons, using: *in addition (to this) as well as besides (this) also*
Your partner agrees or disagrees.

GRAMMAR SUMMARY

Present continuous passive
He is always being asked why he chose postcards.
Are you being photographed on a Greek island?

Cause and effect
Greek postcards have changed *as a result of* Takis' style.
I think he's a director *because of* his hatred of bad films.

17

34

DREAMER OR INSOMNIAC?

It's a fact that we all dream. Some dreams seem to last for hours, others only for seconds. Some of us have fantastic dreams, some amusing dreams, and some of us have unpleasant dreams. Tests in the 1960s showed that these dreams occur within 90-minute cycles, each cycle made up of six stages. In the last stage people experience rapid eye movement, known as REM, and it is in this stage that dreaming takes place. Eighty per cent of people who were woken during this sixth stage could easily remember their dreams. On the other hand, when they were woken during the first five stages (NREM), only seven per cent could describe a dream. However, of these same people woken during the first five phases, 74% were able to recall thinking activity, although they would not call it a dream. Nerys Dee, who has written about dreams in a book called *Your Dreams and What They Mean*, says 'Perhaps during NREM sleep we are sorting out our outer mundane problems, but in REM sleep we are dealing with inner symbolic matters.' She also makes the following comment about the 90-minute cycle: 'It may also account for the reason why insomniacs who wake in the middle of the night find it impossible to get to sleep again for at least an hour and a half. In other words, until they have missed out one complete 90-minute sleep session.'

1 Read the text and say if the following are true or false.
1 Dreaming takes place in all six stages of the 90-minute cycle.
2 Everyone experiences REM.
3 If woken during REM sleep people usually remember dreams.
4 Nerys Dee feels that in all stages of sleep we are finding solutions to conscious problems.
5 Nerys Dee offers a reason why people cannot get to sleep immediately when they wake up in the night.
What is the reason mentioned in *5*?

2 Now complete the chart above with information from the text.

3 The verbs in Column **A** occur in the text. Match them with the meanings in Column **B**.

A	B
made up of	explain why
sort out	find a solution for
deal with	not experience
account for	consisting of
miss out	occur
take place	

Which two have the same meaning?

Now change these sentences to use the verbs:
1 Can you explain why these photographs are missing?
2 Try to find a solution to this problem.
3 She felt that she had not experienced a vital year of her training.
4 Each of my dreams seems to consist of a number of short scenes.
5 The accident occurred at 3 o'clock on Friday.
6 I can't possibly find a solution for your problems: you need to see a doctor.

4 Complete these sentences in your own words, and write a summary of the text.
1 Everyone has dreams; some ____.
2 Although there are six stages in a 90-minute sleep cycle, it is only in the last stage ____.
3 We may sort out different types of ____.
4 It is not until insomniacs have ____.

5 Build up a list of situations/things which you find unpleasant to dream about, and then compare them with other people, like this:
I think it's very unpleasant to dream about ____. What about you?

Do you have recurring dreams (dreams which come again and again)? Tell your partner about them.

6 *Insomniacs find it impossible to get to sleep again for at least an hour and a half.* Imagine you have just had a series of dreams and in those dreams there were some things you found impossible/difficult/easy to do. Make a list of these, using the prompts below. Find out from your partner what these things were, by asking questions, like this:
Did you have a pleasant/amusing/unpleasant dream?
– It was very ____.
Did you find anything impossible/difficult/easy to do in your dream?
– Yes, I found it impossible to ____.
Prompts: wake up, get up, run away from something, speak my own language, fly, win a sports competition etc.

Compare your list with other people.

18

7   Nerys Dee says that in REM sleep we are *dealing with* inner matters. In groups, build up a list of things you feel need to be sorted out or dealt with in your country, for example, unemployment, inflation, crime, strikes etc. Mention things you think it would be difficult to deal with. Write sentences like this:
We feel that the problem of _____ needs to be _____ because _____. We feel that the problem of _____ is difficult to deal with/sort out because _____.

Unlike babies, who sleep 75% of the time, adults sleep for an average of seven hours and twenty minutes. But the truth is that as we grow older we tend to need less sleep. And of course, when we sleep, we dream.

What does the average person dream about? The most common object is a building or part of a building. Then come dreams of streets and gardens, followed by dreams of travelling by car or other means. Swimming, playing games, watching a film and fighting are also common, with men having five times as many aggressive dreams as women. Only 29% of 3,000 dreamers thought they dreamt in colour, although it is possible that everyone does. The memory of colour, like a dream itself, fades quickly on waking.

8   Read the text and answer these questions.
1   Who sleeps more, a young or old person?
2   Are aggressive dreams common in women?
3   Do you dream about the objects listed as common?
4   Do you dream in colour? If so, are you in the majority?
5   Do you think dreams can come true?

9   What are these?
1   Like the Australians, they speak English and live on the opposite side of the world to the UK.
2   Like the Scots, they are British, but unlike the Scots, many of them speak their own language.
3   Like the Germans and the Swiss, they speak German.
4   Like Norway and Sweden, it is in Scandinavia, but it has many more lakes.
5   Like Britain, this country is a European island, but unlike Britain it has many volcanoes.
Try to make up some more questions like these.

Sugar Ray Robinson

One dream that sadly came true, despite the dreamer's efforts to stop the event, happened in 1947, in the boxing ring. Just before a fight with Jimmy Doyle, Sugar Ray Robinson dreamt that during his fight one of his punches killed Doyle. His manager and a priest assured him that dreams did not come true. On that occasion they were wrong.

10   Work in groups. Can you find a good reason for Robinson's dream? Agree on a sentence which summarises your opinion.

11   Nerys Dee gives examples of two types of dreams: the literal dream, which very much reflects the familiar world around us, and the symbolic dream, which reflects our inner world.

Listen to the descriptions of three dreams on tape. Take notes, and then in groups decide which one is symbolic.

12   Discuss the possible meanings of the three dreams in groups, like this:
In the first dream, the man might have been worried about his brakes. – Or the dream might have been a kind of warning.

Make notes about a dream you have had recently and tell the class about it. Make comments about other people's dreams, like this:
You might have wanted/expected/been worried _____.
Were you worried about _____?

Write a description of your dream, or someone else's and write a brief interpretation of what it means.

18

GRAMMAR SUMMARY

Phrasal verbs
Each cycle is made up of six stages.

Adjective + infinitive
I found it impossible to wake up.

Like/unlike
Unlike babies, adults sleep for an average of seven hours and twenty minutes.

Might have **+ past participle**
He might have been worried about his brakes.

NEXT STOP TERMINAL 4

London Heathrow Airport's newest terminal combines the best qualities of the world's top airports.

Before the architects of London's new Terminal 4 building drew a single line at their drawing boards, they took a grand tour of the world's airports to get ideas. When they returned they shared one overriding ambition: to get some natural light into the building. Another message was equally clear: keep it simple. It's a high-tech, functional building with very few frills. In other words, it looks like what it is: a building designed for hard work, handling eight million passengers a year, and built to last.

1 You have just arrived at London Heathrow from Hong Kong on business, and have forgotten to fill in a landing card. Use the information in Resource Text 1a on page 39 to fill in the card below. Now work in pairs. Student **A** uses the landing card to pass through immigration. Student **B** asks him/her questions using the brief in Resource Text 1b.

The first thing that strikes you is the colour scheme. It is silver and terracotta throughout. In fact, like most of the interior design, there are no bright colours. The designers have used lasting and practical colours rather than fashionable ones. What is trendy and smart today would look very out of date ten years from now. These are colours with which the passengers will be happy and relaxed.

Much of the silver is in the heating and ventilation pipes which have been left exposed overhead. The maintenance problems have been greatly reduced by doing away with ceilings.

19

LANDING CARD

Fill this in before disembarking at a British Airport.

Name_____

Nationality_____

Country of embarkation_____

Purpose of visit to U.K._____

Intended length of stay_____

Address in U.K._____

_____

Telephone number_____

2 Stay in your pairs. Student **A**: Use Resource Text 2a to choose your next destination. Then ask airport information (Student **B**) what to do next.
Student **B**: Use the flow chart (2b) to give answers. Use these words: first   next   after that   then

3 An official of the British Airports Authority is giving a guided tour of Terminal 4. Listen to the tape and, looking at the map, decide where the tour begins and where it ends. Then listen again and fill in the blanks on the map.

4 Mrs Petersen is meeting Mr Randolphe from Berlin on BA flight 603 at 4.10 pm. Work in pairs. Look at the roles in Resource Text 3 on page 39 and act out a meeting between them.

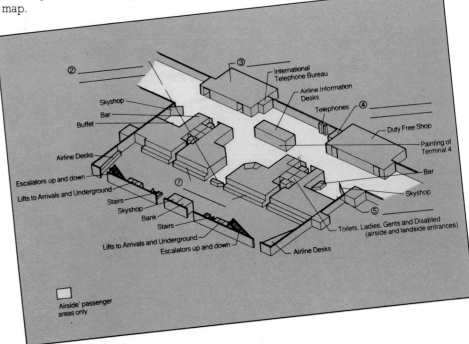

Terminal 4 is radically different from the usual airport design because there are no separate departure gates. The reason is that stretched jumbos will be flying out of the terminal, and the building would have needed to be two or three times its present length if they had built a separate room for each gate. Instead there is one gigantic lounge, a quarter of a mile in length, which serves all the aircraft gates. And you can actually see the gate numbers. They are written in three-foot high neon figures.

The terminal will handle all of British Airways' intercontinental flights, including Concorde, and there are 64 British Airways check-in desks. The aim is to get people checked in as quickly as possible so that they can relax afterwards.

The main departure lounge runs the entire 650-metre length of Terminal 4, so that passengers have panoramic views of the apron and the aircraft taking off from the main runway beyond. The windows are well placed to provide daylight and entertaining views of air traffic movements. These big, glazed areas are important because you're not losing touch with the things you know and understand. People feel claustrophobic in airports. But if they can see sky and trees and they can see things happening outside, they may feel more relaxed.

Inside the great hall there are bars and tax- and duty-free shops. In the huge tax-free facilities you can buy perfumes, jewellery, cameras and so on. Both of these shops have been decorated to make you feel more as though you are shopping in Harrods than in an airport terminal. There are also newspaper stands and places to eat. Here a passenger may relax. Beyond the glass, mechanics and technicians work hard to make the aircraft ready. Tables and chairs spill out from the buffet areas onto the concourse, creating a continental atmosphere where you can relax and watch the world go by as you wait for your flight.

5   Work in pairs. Student **A:** You are flying to New Delhi on British Airways. Decide how much your luggage weighs, whether you are carrying any restricted goods, how many seats you want together, where you want to sit, and whether you have any special requirements (cot for baby, special menu etc).
Student **B:** You are a member of British Airways ground staff. Refer to the guidelines in Resource Text 4 on page 40 and interview Student **A.**

6   Look at the duty-free regulations in Resource Text 5 on page 40 and then listen to the explanation on tape. You and your partner are customs officers, doing spot checks on people coming through the green gate. Decide if any of the following people have duty to pay.
1   Mrs Kirk is bringing the following goods, duty and tax paid, from Singapore: 150 Benson and Hedges, king size, 75 cigarillos, four litres of still table wine and three fl oz of Ma Griffe, as gifts.

2   Monsieur and Madame Beaumont are carrying 400 grammes of tobacco, purchased in a special shop in Paris, 200 duty-free Gauloises, one litre of Calvados and one litre of Rémy Martin, and three presentation boxes of perfume totalling five fl oz, and fifteen fl oz of toilet water.
3   Manuel Gonzales is visiting his married daughter in Birmingham and has brought three toy aeroplanes (£3.50 each), a watch for his daughter (£12.50) and a silk tie for his son-in-law (£10.00), all purchased on the plane from Barcelona. He is also bringing in 50 duty-free cigars, two litres of red table wine and two litres of Spanish sherry.

7   Look at the symbols in Resource Text 6 on page 40 and, in groups, decide what you think they mean. Check your answers, then decide where they might go on the map.

8   Read the descriptions of Terminal 4 under the photographs and find reasons for the following features. Discuss each one with a partner and decide what you think of the idea.
1   High tech/functional/no frills
2   No bright colours
3   No separate departure gates
4   One long departure lounge
5   Exposed pipework
6   Large areas of glass
7   Large number of check-in desks
8   Three-foot neon gate numbers
9   Checking people in quickly
10   Tables and chairs on the concourse

9   Now read the extracts from an article in an in-flight magazine (Resource Text 7). What things does the author say which do not agree with the advertisement on these two pages? Take notes and compare your findings in groups.

1a

Name _GIOVANNI FRANCONI_

Nationality _ITALIAN_

Address _BLOCK 4, 7/F, QUEEN'S COURT_

83, WELLINGTON STREET CENTRAL HONG KONG

Occupation _COMMERCIAL BUYER_
Profession

Place of birth _MILAN, ITALY_
Lieu de naissance

Date of birth _18 JUNE 1961_
Date de naissance

Residence _HONG KONG_
Residence

Height _1.78_____ m _____ m
Taille

Distinguishing marks _____
Signes particuliers

CHILDREN _ENFANTS_

Name Nom   **Date of birth** Date de naissance   **Sex** Sexe

_____

Usual Signature of bearer
Signature du titulaire

Usual signature of spouse
Signature de son epouse

19

2a

Flight Departures

AIRLINE	DESTINATION	FLIGHT NO	DEPARTURE TIME	TERMINAL
British Airways	Edinburgh	BA 4752	11.10	1
British Airways	Pisa	BA 528	11.15	1
British Airways	Helsinki	BA 668	11.15	1
Aer Lingus	Dublin	EI 157	11.30	1
SAS	Stockholm	SK 526	11.10	2
Lufthansa	Bremen	LH 047	11.25	2
Air France	Paris	AF 811	11.30	2
Pan Am	New York	PA 101	11.00	3
Air Canada	Montreal	AC 861	12.00	3
Gulf Air	Muscat	GS 016	12.00	3
British Airways	Miami	BA 293	11.30	4
British Airways	Pittsburgh	BA 219	11.55	4
British Airways	Amsterdam	BA 410	12.00	4

1b Brief for Immigration Officers

1 Check country of origin/embarkation
2 Check how long they are planning to stay in the UK
3 Establish purpose of visit
4 Get them to repeat UK address/telephone number
5 Ask them to produce ticket for next stage of journey

2b

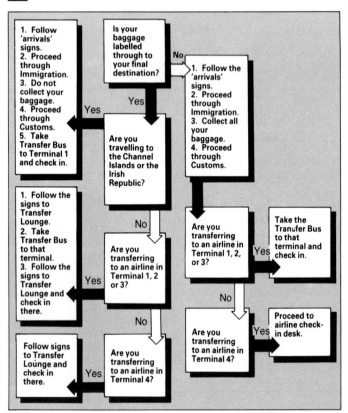

3a

You are Mr Randolphe and you are looking for Mrs Petersen. She will have a sign showing your name, but she has spelt Randolphe without the 'e'. You left home at 3 o'clock and your flight was on time, but it was dreadful. The plane was very full and there was no leg room. The weather in Berlin was bright and sunny when you left (15°C), but you hit bad weather on the way across. You want to know where you will be staying and when you will be meeting Mr Petersen.

3b

You are Mrs Petersen and you are meeting Mr Randolphe. He is coming to see your husband on business and you have never met before. You will be holding a sign with his name. You make polite conversation by asking how the flight was, when he left home/Berlin, what the weather was like (the weather in London is terrible – it's rainy and cold). You take him up in the lift to the second floor of the car park and ask him to wait there while you get the car. You are going to take him to his hotel and your husband will be meeting him at 7.30 pm for drinks and then taking him to dinner at the Café de Paris.

4 Check-in procedure for British Airways ground staff

1 Ask how many are together.
2 Ask to see his/her/their ticket(s).
3 Ask to see his/her/their passport(s).
4 Ask if they want smoking or non-smoking sections.
5 Ask if they have any special requirements.
6 Ask them if they are carrying any restricted goods (non-safety matches, aerosols over $\frac{1}{2}$ litre each – total 2 litres, gas cylinders, paints, thinners, instruments containing magnets).
7 Give them tags for their luggage and ask them to put their bags on the scales (weight limit 15 kilos/excess charge is about £11.00 per kilo).
8 Ask them if they have any cabin luggage (cabin luggage must be able to fit under the seat).

5

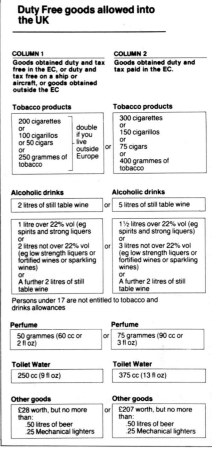

Duty Free goods allowed into the UK

COLUMN 1 Goods obtained duty and tax free in the EC, or duty and tax free on a ship or aircraft, or goods obtained outside the EC		COLUMN 2 Goods obtained duty and tax paid in the EC.
Tobacco products		**Tobacco products**
200 cigarettes or 100 cigarillos or 50 cigars or 250 grammes of tobacco	double if you live outside Europe	300 cigarettes or 150 cigarillos or 75 cigars or 400 grammes of tobacco
Alcoholic drinks		**Alcoholic drinks**
2 litres of still table wine	or	5 litres of still table wine
1 litre over 22% vol (eg spirits and strong liquers) or 2 litres not over 22% vol (eg low strength liquers or fortified wines or sparkling wines) or A further 2 litres of still table wine		1½ litres over 22% vol (eg spirits and strong liquers) or 3 litres not over 22% vol (eg low strength liquers or fortified wines or sparkling wines) or A further 2 litres of still table wine
Persons under 17 are not entitled to tobacco and drinks allowances		
Perfume		**Perfume**
50 grammes (60 cc or 2 fl oz)	or	75 grammes (90 cc or 3 fl oz)
Toilet Water		**Toilet Water**
250 cc (9 fl oz)		375 cc (13 fl oz)
Other goods		**Other goods**
£28 worth, but no more than: .50 litres of beer .25 Mechanical lighters	or	£207 worth, but no more than: .50 litres of beer .25 Mechanical lighters

7

WINDOW ON A NEW WORLD
Nick Hanna Reports

British Airways is switching all its intercontinental flights, including Concorde, plus short-haul routes to Paris and Amsterdam, to Terminal 4 and will be sharing it with KLM, Air Malta and NLM.

BA has spent £14m on equipping the new terminal, and there have been many criticisms of it. It is very like being inside a large aircraft hangar, because of the size of the enormous concourse and the fact that all the heating and ventilation pipework has been left exposed, or "expressed", as they say. This is in line with current hi-tech fashion and of course the two most famous examples of this are the Beaubourg Centre in Paris and the new Lloyd's building in London. These are successful because the exposed services are in a variety of colours, styles and shapes which are pleasing to the eye. In Terminal 4 this idea has been converted to vast, silver air-conditioning ducts hanging down from the ceiling.

The huge pre-departure concourse seems to have been designed so that the airline passenger will spend the maximum amount of money while waiting for a flight. The designers say that they had two objectives: to allow the airport to make money from non-flight activities, and to make the huge building, which covers one million square feet, attractive to people. They have used trees and sculpture to help fulfil the second objective. The lavish duty- and tax-free outlets will fulfil the first.

The expensive looking pink and grey marble tax-free shops are very different from the plastic looking finishes in other parts of the terminal.

Immediately after clearing passport control and security, and entering the main concourse, passengers meet an enormous solid grey wall dead ahead of them. This would have been the perfect spot for wall-to-ceiling glass. It could have been a marvellous sight for passengers entering the concourse – a unique opportunity to provide an enormous view of the world's busiest airport. Instead there is an enormous 20ft × 8ft painting of the Terminal 4 building itself.

Two enormous duty-free shops block the immediate view of the airport. And the walls facing the airport are about 30ft high, but instead of floor-to-ceiling glass, only one third of this is glazed. And even then not all the way along the concourse. So you're left with a series of small 10ft high windows, set in groups of a dozen, surrounded by acres and acres of panelling. Another thing is that at T4 many of the windows have their view blocked by enormous airbridges made out of yellow corrugated metal.

When you are sitting in the central cafeteria, instead of being able to have a drink and enjoy a fantastic panorama of the airport, all you get is a view of the duty- and tax-free shops.

The BAA's own architect, Maurice Kenfield, admits that there aren't any panoramas and that the terminal has been designed so that there is as little natural daylight as possible, because they can control passengers' moods more effectively with artificial light.

I suggested to one of the designers that the seats were extremely uncomfortable and he admitted that they had been

designed that way. 'People (one hopes) aren't going to be there for that long, and we needed to get in as many seats as we could. Half an hour is the longest you should have to stay there.'

There are 5,000 of these seats, which have metal tubular frames. There is disposable upholstery to allow easy replacement. Another requirement was visibility – so you can see from a long way whether a bag has been left behind. Nowhere is the word *comfort* mentioned. You can't lean back or stretch out in them, and they don't even have armrests. They are also too low, and disabled and elderly people will have trouble getting out of them.

Food is provided by a large American catering service and consists mostly of sausage rolls, pizzas, hot dogs, stuffed croissants and ice creams. There is one silver-service restaurant, but it only seats 40 people and it is landside – outside the departure lounge. There is also a cocktail bar with a piano player, but this is also landside. If the BAA's aim is to get people checked in as quickly as possible so that they can relax afterwards, why have such an unusual and original feature as a piano bar before check in?

The designers' main objective has been to cut down passenger tensions in modern air travel and create a new kind of environment for the new breed of traveller. At Terminal 4 they've tried to make the things you choose to do – like spending money – more relaxed.

From Business Traveller/April 1986

6

Answers to Exercise 1.
Meanings of symbols commonly found in airports
1 information 2 banks and currency exchange 3 baggage security 4 post office 5 public telephones 6 restaurants and grills 7 licensed bars 8 toilets for the disabled 9 taxis 10 car hire

19

In so many words

1 Complete these words:

li __ __ ly; ch __ __ fly; w __ __ el __;

va __ __ __ d; art __ __ __ __ ial

2 Now use the words above in these sentences:

1 Spanish is a . . . . used language.

2 The price of a telephone call is . . . . . . to go up next year.

3 A well known . . . . language is Esperanto.

4 Latin is . . . . . . used for medicine.

5 The number of languages in India is very . . . .

3 Look at the following languages and make sentences, like this:

German is spoken in Germany but I think it is also spoken in Austria.

1 English ....

....

2 French ....

....

3 Spanish ....

....

4 Portuguese ....

....

5 Chinese ....

....

6 Arabic ....

....

4a Put the following words and phrases in the correct column.

likely to   may   will probably   should   will   is certain to   might   could

possibility	probability	certainty

b Write five sentences about what you are likely to do next year, like this:

Next year I could be working in Malaysia.

5 Complete these sentences:

1 I'm not likely to ....

2 I'm unlikely to ....

3 My sister/brother/cousin probably won't ....

6 Complete these sentences, like this:

If they'd watched the match, they'd probably have enjoyed it.

1 If he'd caught the train he'd probably ....

2 If ....

she'd quite likely ....

3 If she'd spent less money, she'd be able to ....

4 If they'd learnt the language, it's likely that they

would ....

7 Without looking at the text in the Coursebook, rearrange the following sentences into the correct order:

1 A Punjabi from the north, and a Madrasi from the south will converse quite frequently in English. . . .

2 It is hard to believe that there are so many areas where people speak not one language but two or even three.   . . .

3 Poor farmers on the Thai-Cambodian border are likely to speak two languages.   . . .

4 But it is in the world's border areas where multilingualism is often found.   . . .

1

Call me mister!

1 Complete these words:

ex_____ssion; dis_____fort;

f_____al; alt_____ati___;

re_____ship;

si_____cant

2 Now use the words above in these sentences:

1 Nobody really likes to feel ...., especially when they are on holiday

2 I'm afraid you'll have to wear a suit. The party is

rather ....

3 When people cry a lot it's often an .... of anxiety

4 Many married people maintain an excellent

.... for years

5 Do you think there is a .... difference between your performance and mine?

6 I'm afraid you'll have to do it. There's no ....

3 Complete these sentences, using *had been -ing*, like this:

His clothes were very dirty because he'd been working in the garden for hours when she arrived.

1 She was out of breath because .... when he phoned.

2 Because .... nobody would believe her later when she said she hadn't stolen it.

3 He put on a lot of weight because .... when he was in hospital.

4 The children were unhappy because ....

before it started to rain ....

5 Because .... everyone was surprised when he left the job.

4 Complete the following sentences in your own words, like this:

It's impossible to relax with them.

1 It's impossible to ....

2 It's very hard to ....

3 I think it's very dangerous to ....

4 Don't you think's necessary to ....?

5 Wouldn't it be nice to ....?

5 Match columns **A** and **B**, then make sentences like this:

They had been living in Washington for nine months before/when they saw the President.

	A	B
1	They/work for several hours	find/a shop
2	They/learn English for several years	speak/any Chinese
3	They/live in Taiwan for four years	stop/for coffee
4	They/walk for quite a few miles	reach/their destination
5	They/run the business for four years	meet/a person from Britain
6	They/fly for six hours	make/a profit

6 Complete these sentences in your own words, like this:

It was so hot that . . .: *It was so hot that you could fry an egg on the road.*

1 The train was so fast that ....

2 The party was so formal that ....

3 We were so bored at their house that ....

4 She spoke so softly that ....

5 Although they were very good friends she lived so

far away that ....

2

A matter of manners

1 Rearrange these letters to make words from unit 13:

beviouhar .... lycontsant .... vilisdeci

.... embassarr .... cpoy ....

2 Now use the words above in these sentences:

1 I must say that I think his .... is really awful.

2 Did you know that he talks ......? He never stops.

3 He was very worried that he would .... his friends.

4 Some people always .... the actions of others.

5 Some people with a lot of money and advantages

are not nearly as .... as people without these opportunities.

3 Use the table to write ten sentences:

A	B	C	D	E	F	G
If	he she they	had	learnt the language arrived earlier known about the weather been better informed telephoned in time	he she they	might have	....

4 Change the sentences you wrote for exercise 3 into the negative, like this:

If they had learnt the language they would have enjoyed themselves.
If they hadn't learnt the language they wouldn't have enjoyed themselves.

5 Rearrange these words to make sentences:

1 need/have/not/come/early/you/so ....

....

2 we/should/be/not/late ....

....

3 have/might/her/he/told/yet/not ....

....

4 if/we/worked/might/been/have/harder/had/

successful/we ....

....

5 she/asleep/injection/been/was/because/had/she/an/

given ....

....

6 When you arrived home yesterday, several things hadn't been done. Write sentences like this:

beds: *The beds hadn't been made.*

1 dishes ....

....

2 carpets ....

....

3 food ....

....

4 children's toys ....

....

7 Give advice to a friend about how to behave in public, like this:

I think you should let old people get on the bus first.
I think you shouldn't smoke in crowded restaurants.

1 ....

....

2 ....

....

3 ....

....

4 ....

....

Shrinking World

1 Complete these words:

cul＿＿＿e;　com＿＿＿＿＿tions;

conc＿＿＿＿＿on;　backg＿＿＿nd;

sim＿＿＿riti＿s

2 Now use the words above in these sentences:

1 There are often ...... when you travel abroad.

2 I would like to have more ...... about France.

3 The ...... of ancient Greece fascinates me.

4 Do you see any ...... between the two languages?

5 It was clever the way the detective reached his ...... about the motive.

3 Complete these sentences:

1 ....,
but I myself don't like it.

2 ....,
but I myself disagree with him.

3 ....,
but I myself have never been there.

4 ....,
but I myself can't stand it.

4 Write the sentences that go before these sentences, like this:

Don't tell us what to do.　We want to decide for ourselves.

1 ....
He only wants it for himself.

2 ....
She said she wanted to try it for herself.

3 ....
They said they would go by themselves.

4 ....
I think we don't need it for ourselves.

5 Complete these sentences, using *it's possible to* or *one can*, like this:

If you know the owner, *it's possible to get a discount.*
If it's an emergency, *one can get a dental appointment easily.*

1 If you stand at the top of the Eiffel Tower ....

2 In London ....

3 If you travel by car ....

4 If you stay in cheap hotels ....

5 Knowledge of another language means ....

6 Living in a country for a long time ....

6 Someone is staying in your house while you are on holiday. Using the prompts below, write down some suggestions for him so that he knows what to do if anything goes wrong. For example:

tax inspector might telephone:　*The tax inspector might telephone while I'm away. If that happens tell him I'm on holiday.*

1 refrigerator might break down ....

....

2 washing machine may leak ....

....

3 telephone may not work ....

....

4 car may not start ....

....

5 doorbell might not work ....

....

4

44

Men and women . . . women and men

1 Complete the following sentences, like this:

If I hear noises in the night, I tell *myself* that it's *only the wind*.

1 All of them escaped quickly from the burning

   house, and thought to ....

   afterwards that ....

2 He paid only £3000 for the car, telling ....

3 At last she finished work, after one of the hardest

   days in her life, and said to ....

   that ....

4 When I find I want to eat too much, I warn ....

2 Write five dialogues using the words below to make the questions.

angry   anxious   confident   happy   tired

A: Why was Roger so ....?

B: It must have been because ....

3 Complete the following sentences, giving reasons why Gert and Dagmar have left each other.

I think it must have been because ....

I think it might have been because ....

I think it could have been because ....

4 You are arranging to share a flat with two other people who you don't know very well. You decide to make some rules about what the three of you should and shouldn't do.

Write the six rules below.

1 ....

   should ....

2 ....

   should not ....

3 ....

   should not ....

4 ....

   should ....

5 ....

   should not ....

6 ....

   should ....

5 Without looking at the Coursebook, rearrange the following sentences into the correct order:

1 It's always money.   . . .

2 She's more tired now than she used to be.   . . .

3 Most of the time she's tired.   . . .

4 However, he says they can't afford it.   . . .

5 If they had a washing machine it would be easier.
                                                        . . .

6 Complete the following dialogues, like this:

A   I wonder why the dog's barking?
B   *It must be because there's someone outside.*

1 A   I wonder why the train's so late?

  B   ....

2 A   Do you know why he doesn't speak English?

  B   ....

3 A   I wonder why they always argue?

  B   ....

4 A   Do you know why the hotel's so expensive?

  B   ....

5 A   Do you know why she's so difficult to talk to?

  B   ....

The natural way

1 Complete these words:

pr__ess____al;   sp____fic;

h__lth___;   ca__m;

proc____

2 Now use the words above in these sentences:

1 Yes, he earns his money playing football. He's a

. . . .

2 The law says exactly when you can and can't park

here. It's very . . . .

3 I don't really understand how it works. Can you

explain the . . . .

4 He hardly ever gets angry. In fact, he's a very

. . . . person.

5 He looks much . . . . since he stopped smoking.

3 Complete these sentences, like this:

I wouldn't have bought it if it'd been owned by a salesman.

1 She wouldn't have done it unless she'd felt . . . .

2 She wouldn't have phoned you unless it'd been . . . .

3 He wouldn't have written it if they hadn't . . . .

4 I wouldn't have known about it if she hadn't . . . .

5 He wouldn't have seen it if they hadn't . . . .

4 Now go back to the five sentences in exercise three, and say what the word *it* means in each sentence, like this:

In the first sentence, I think the word 'it' means a car.

5 Complete these sentences, like this:

He resigned from the company. It must have been because he didn't get a rise.

1 She went to bed early. It must have been

because . . . .

2 They drove off very quickly. It must have been

because . . . .

3 The railway men went on strike. It must have been

because . . . .

4 The hospitals were full. It must have been

because . . . .

5 The roads were flooded. It must have been

because . . . .

6 Without looking at the text in the Coursebook, rearrange these sentences into the correct order:

1 In the event of a child having a temperature, we know that sometimes we can calm him or her by smoothing the brow.   . . .

2 We also all know people who respond better to one doctor than another.   . . .

3 We still retain some examples of it in our everyday lives.   . . .

4 We say the doctors have a good beside manner.   . . .

5 Then the fever may go down and the child will be able to sleep.   . . .

7 Write a sign for a hotel bedroom explaining what to do if there is a fire. Begin *In case of . . .*

8 Write another sign, this time explaining how to get a doctor. Begin *In the event of . . .*

Food for thought

1

1 Name something that makes you anxious. . . . .

2 Name any illnesses or diseases you or a friend has suffered from. . . . .

3 The text talks about children behaving in abnormal ways. What kind of behaviour do you think is abnormal? . . . .

2 The opposites of these words occur in unit 7. What are they?

accept . . . . exceptional . . . . . . careless

. . . . the former . . . . . . decline . . . .

3 Make excuses, like this:

Go to a party:
finish/my work
I'm afraid I can't go because I won't have finished my work.

1 Go to a formal party:
bring/the correct clothes . . . .

. . . .

2 Go out with friends:
complete/housework . . . .

. . . .

3 Go to the theatre:
have time/to get a babysitter . . . .

. . . .

4 Go home at 6:
make/all my telephone calls . . . .

. . . .

5 Help a friend (Robert):
done/my own work . . . .

. . . .

4 Use the statements in column **A** to help you to match columns **B**, **C** and **D**. Then make sentences, like this:

He enjoyed the hotel: *He stayed in the hotel in spite of the expense*

	A	B	C	D
1	He was angry he missed the train.	stay/hotel		the rain
2	They didn't meet.	lose/football match		he complained
3	He finished the meal	ate/meal	in spite of the fact that	he left early
4	She was pleased with her exam results	see their friends	because of the fact that	her hard work
5	They played badly in wet weather	catch/train		they telephoned many times
6	He enjoyed the hotel	pass/exam		the expense

5 Here are five different people, each with a different profession. Make one sentence about each person, to show what they will have done in their jobs for the period given, like this:

Brigitte: personal assistant (one year from now)
Brigitte will have become a personal assistant by 1991

1 Karin: dentist (three years from now)

2 Lars: pilot (one year from now)

3 Erik: cook (two weeks from now)

4 Henri: train driver (one month from now)

5 Diego: car salesman (one month from now)

6 The following people suffer from medical problems. Write about the possible causes, like this:

Jane/really bad back/strain/move the furniture
Jane's got a really bad back. I think she might have strained it when she was moving the furniture.

1 Tom/awful cold/catch/work in the rain

2 Dick/bad case of hepatitis/get/visit friends in Asia

3 Bob/very painful elbow/get/play tennis

4 Janet/very sore knee/hurt/run in the race

5 My grandfather/very poor eyesight/damage/repair watches for a living

7

Paradise Lost?

1 Complete these words:

vo__g__; imp__ss__on;

extra____inari__; fra_____;

com_____t____

2 Now use the words above in the sentences:

1 Wrap it up carefully, please. It's extremely ....

   2 Her ...... of the new manager was that he wasn't very competent.

3 People who live in small ...... have few secrets.

4 Pretty? I thought the sunset at Sounion was ...... beautiful.

5 Because the weather has been so stormy, the

   Milnes were extremely relieved when the ...... was over and they docked at Southampton.

3 Complete these sentences, like this:

If the sun hadn't been so strong he would've gone out immediately.

1 If I hadn't been in a hurry then ....

2 If she hadn't been so late then ....

3 If the colonists of the United States hadn't been so

   ....

4 If the road hadn't been so icy ....

5 If the wind hadn't been so bad ....

4 Rearrange these words to make sentences, which contain the expressions *needn't have been*, and *shouldn't have been.*

1 you/been/not/so/early/need/have ....

   ....

2 careless/should/you/so/been/have/not ....

   ....

3 they/not/have/need/been/generous/so ....

   ....

4 we/have/not/should/been/informal/so ....

   ....

5 you/should/have/so/been/not/late ....

   ....

5 Now give reasons for each of the statements in exercise 4, using *because, as* or *since*, like this:

You need not have been so early since the meal isn't ready yet.

6 Write a paragraph of about fifty to seventy five words, saying what the rainforests are and where you are likely to find them.

7 Write two sentences about your own life, like this:

If I hadn't had a good teacher, I wouldn't have passed the exam.

8 Without looking at the text in the Coursebook, rearrange these sentences into the correct order:

1 The gas rises and traps the sun's heat in much the same ways as the glass of a greenhouse.   . . .

2 Worse still, the climate is likely to change as the trees are no longer there to absorb the carbon dioxide.   . . .

3 In the years to come perhaps people will say that much of our forests needn't have been destroyed. . . .

4 When trees disappear from the land, the water sources suddenly disappear.   . . .

5 The land itself washes away, either becoming very poor or complete desert.   . . .

Acid rain

1 Do you know what these are? Use your dictionaries, if necessary.

smog fog an oil slick chemical pollution
nuclear fallout smoke

2 Now complete the following sentences, which use the words above:

1 People are so worried by nuclear fallout that ....

2 In Norway, chemical pollution ....

3 An oil slick happens when ....

4 There is no smoke without ....

5 Fog often occurs ....

6 Smog occurs in certain weather conditions,

   when ....

3 Match columns **A** and **B** then write sentences using *as a result of this, as a result, because of this, consequently, as a consequence.*

A	**B**
1 Huge amounts of snow fell over the north part of the country	Many fish have died
2 There was a nuclear accident at Chernobyl	They were caught at home with no food
3 There has been a great deal of sulphur pollution in the Scandinavian lakes	Other animals have suffered
4 Most people were unprepared	A large quantity of fruit and food became polluted
5 Many of the fish died	A lot of people couldn't leave their homes

4 Answer these questions about your country:

1 What are the most heavily polluted areas? ....

2 Do you have forest areas and where are they? ....

3 Do you have large lakes and where are they? ....

4 What are the names of your big rivers, and are they

   free from pollution? ....

5 Complete these sentences:

1 The way people learn is affected by ....

   ....

   2 The way people think is affected by ....

   ....

3 The way people make friends is affected by ....

   ....

4 The way in which people live is affected by ....

   ....

   5 The way people travel is affected by ....

   ....

6 Complete these sentences:

1 People drive too fast. As a result, ...

2 The weather this winter has been awful. As a result,

   ....

3 Many of the fish are dead. This is due to ....

4 Some people have moved out of the big cities. This

   is due to ....

7 Give advice to a friend, making sentences using the words below, like this:

Your health might be improved by eating less fat.

1	teeth			strengthen
2	body	might	weaken
3	a weight problem	could	improve
4	eyesight	will	damage
5	health		help

49

9

Warriors of the rainbow

1 Complete this table:

Verb	Noun
revolve	
destroy	
reverse	
demand	
organise	

2 Write questions and answers, like this:
to the Challenger space shuttle/explode
Do you know what happened to the Challenger space shuttle?
Yes, it exploded in space.

1 in 1945/second world war ....

....

2 in 1969/land/moon ....

....

3 Titanic/sink/Atlantic Ocean ....

....

4 in 1492/Columbus sail/America ....

....

5 in Mexico/earthquake ....

....

3 Change these questions, like this:

What's for tea? (he): *He wants to know what's for tea.*
What're you doing? (they): *They want to know what you're doing.*

1 What's your name? (she) ....

....

2 What's the time? (he) ....

....

3 What can I do to help you? (she) ....

....

4 What kind of car have you got? (he) ....

....

5 What's the name of this kind of fish? (he) ....

....

4 Change these questions in the same way:

1 When is it going to start? (she) ....

....

2 Why is she coming? (they) ....

....

3 How are we getting them? (they) ....

....

4 Where is it going to be held? (he) ....

....

5 Who is going to arrange it? (she) ....

....

5 Write out the following numbers in words:

30,003 ....

14,567 ....

126,890 ....

2,347,801 ....

401,892,367 ....

6 Make sentences from the columns below, like this:

I'm sorry to say that your car won't be repaired until next week.

A	B	C	D	E
I'm glad to say I'm sorry to say	that your	carpet car clothes lawn house book bicycle parcel food	cut return cook repair mend clean send paint be ready	by . . . before . . until. . .

Animalspeak

1 What are these words from Unit 26?

1 The opposite of shallow is . . . . . .

2 His . . . . . . are B.I.L., which stand for Brian Ian Lane.

3 If you are worried about something you say you are . . . .

4 We need to increase understanding between people, not . . . . it.

5 If we don't see people for a long time, we often don't . . . . them.

2 Write the names of some animals that:

1 roar . . . .

2 sing . . . .

3 chirp . . . .

4 have feathers . . . .

5 have tails . . . .

6 have spines . . . .

3 Complete the following sentences, like this:

I walked down the street but realised I/watch/by
I walked down the street but realised I was being watched by two men.

1 I saw a large black box which/carry/by . . . .

. . . .

2 There was a woman in the shop who/see to/by . . . .

. . . .

3 I watched two men outside the police station who/ take to . . . .

. . . .

4 They told us they/take out to . . . .

. . . .

5 The parcel/send to . . . .

. . . .

4 Make sentences using *as well as*, *in addition to* or *besides*, like this:

Paris/Lyon (go): *We went to Paris. As well as this we went to Lyon. We went to Lyon as well as Paris.*

1 Madrid/Toledo (visit) . . . .

. . . .

2 London/Wales (go) . . . .

. . . .

3 Buckingham Palace/Westminster Abbey (see) . . . .

. . . .

4 Monkeys/Elephants (hear) . . . .

. . . .

5 Use the prompts below to write sentences using *in order to* or *to*, like this:

go to university
be a doctor
In order to go to university it's necessary to pass examinations.
To be a good doctor you've got to go to university.

1 study law
be a barrister . . . .

. . . .

2 get a passport
visit the USSR . . . .

. . . .

3 pass your driving test

drive a car . . . .

. . . .

4 pass an eye test

be a pilot . . . .

. . . .

11

The living department store

1 Complete these words:

af___r_; pr_____us_y;

aff___t; de___g_;

_ua ___t_; c_____r__bl_

2 Now use the words above in these sentences:

1 I think it's really important to have a . . . . living room.

2 It's stupid to buy things you can't . . . .

3 I'm living in Rotterdam now, but . . . . . . I lived in Antwerp.

4 Don't you think you should talk about the . . . . of the service, rather than the cost?

5 The Italians . . . . really good shoes.

6 If you continue smoking like that it's bound to

. . . . your health.

3 Write six sentences about a room in your house, describing the location of pieces of furniture, like this:

In my living room there is a large sofa in the middle of the room, and near it . . .

Use: next to   beside   in front of   just behind   to the right/left of   in the middle   not far from

4 Ask questions that are suitable for the following situations:

1 You want to get to the nearest department store.

2 You want to know where the children's department is.

3 You don't like the design of a clock and ask to see some more.

4 You want to buy some clothes. You have a limited amount of money and the salesman brings you an item which is too much. Ask to see something else.

5 Write three short paragraphs comparing some of the stores in your town.

Use: better than   worse than   the worst
more/less expensive than
and these: considerably   quite a lot   rather   a little

6 Check on the meaning of *somewhat* and *a great deal* in a dictionary and then write sentences using these ideas, like this:

more modern: *Los Angeles is a great deal more modern than Boston.*
less creative: *Their designs were somewhat less creative than I expected.*

1 easier ....

....

2 less expensive ....

....

3 more interesting ....

....

4 less comfortable ....

....

7 Use the information in the chart to write sentences like this:

Peter/Venice/live/1983: *Peter used to live in Venice but he left there in 1983.*

1 Roger/Rome/work/1978 ....

....

2 Liz/Brighton/live/1984 ....

....

3 Beatrice/Dublin/work/1979 ....

....

4 Rhona and Paul/Paris/live/1985 ....

....

12

Opting out

1 Rearrange these letters to make words from unit 8:

epa .... gebbcaa .... ecultte ....

roulf .... plafircee .... rugas ....

maj ....

2 Twenty years ago the following people were all quite young, and all had ideas about what they wanted to be when they had jobs. Make sentences using the clues, like this:

Jack: Someone who operates on you in a hospital (s__ge__)
Jack was going to be a surgeon but he didn't become one.

1 Jo: Someone who mends your car (me____nic)

2 Bill: Someone who flies an aircraft (_____t)

3 Christine: Someone who works in a laboratory (res ____ch__)

4 Alice: Someone who works in a hospital (nu____)

5 Xavier: Someone who goes out to sea to catch fish (____erm__)

3 Complete the following sentences in your own words using *going to*:

1 She said she was going to ....,

but she didn't get here till 10.30.

2 He told me he wasn't ....,

but he didn't go to bed until after midnight.

3 They told me ....,

but they watched the news and the late film.

4 ....,

but he ate a lot, anyway.

5 ....,

but she didn't seem ill when we saw her.

4 Complete the following sentences in your own words:

1 ....

Nevertheless, he does earn a lot of money.

2 He likes his children very much. Nevertheless, ...

....

3 His grandfather is seventy four years old. On the

other hand, ...

....

4 ....

On the other hand, he does speak Spanish quite well.

5 A friend of yours has left his job in the city and is now living on a farm. Match columns **A** and **B**, then make sentences like this:

There's a chicken house, and also there are chickens running around the garden.

		A	B
	1	a chicken house (and also)	no buses/run/weekend
	2	a family of four on the same farm (and)	cats/run around
	3	a stable for the cows (and)	apple trees/grow behind the farm
There's	4	a pear tree next to the house (and)	some wait/to be picked in the fields
There are	5	problems getting to the nearest town on Saturday (because)	a lot/wait/to be done on Saturdays
	6	dogs (and)	another family/live nearby
	7	a lot of vegetables in the barn (and)	large barn/stand close by
	8	a lot of work in the week (but also)	chickens/run around the garden

6 Write a short paragraph beginning *I want my children to learn . . .*

13

53

Festivals of Light

1 Complete these words:

oppor_____; exp_____nce;

___nder ____l; en_____us;

con _____ction; con_____

2 Now use the words above in these sentences:

1 Visiting different countries can often be an amazing

. . . .

2 My boss is . . . . . . He's 1.90m tall and weighs 150kg.

3 What does the work . . . . . . of?

4 People say that the . . . . . . of the pyramids took years.

5 I've never had the . . . . . . to travel.

6 It would be . . . . . . to visit the Far East.

3 Change the following sentences, like this:

Besides inheriting £100,000, he won £5,000 in the football pools.
He inherited £100,000 but besides this he won £5,000 in the football pools.

1 As well as getting a letter from Ron he got one from Nora.

....

2 In addition to having a headache, he felt extremely tired.

....

3 Besides being good at tennis, she was an excellent basketball player.

....

4 As well as having a lot of work to do at the office she also had a lot of housework.

....

5 In addition to having no money he had a lot of debts.

....

6 Besides speaking French and German he spoke Chinese and Japanese.

....

4 Talk about your own life. Make sentences like this:

My main job is to visit people with problems. Besides this I have to keep records.

1 ....

Besides this I have to ....

2 Besides ....

I have to ....

3 ....

As well as this I've been to ....

4 As well as ....

I also ....

5 ....

In addition to this I lived for ....

6 In addition to learning ....

I learnt ....

5 What can you remember about your childhood? Make sentences like this:

As a child, I remember being frightened of the dark.

1 As a child, I remember . . . . . .ing ....

2 When I was younger, I can remember . . . . . .ing

....

3 When my brother/sister was younger I can

remember him/her . . . . . .ing ....

4 As a child, I remember my parents . . . . . .ing ....

5 When we were in . . . ., I remember . . . . . .ing

14

54

A holiday with a difference

1 Rearrange these letters to make words from unit 28:

advio .... gicldunin .... ylghohturo

.... ixcteo .... riuqpctusee ....

2 Now use the words above in these sentences:

1 The rent is £85 a week, ... electricity.

2 Remember to check your work .... before handing it in.

3 Can't you try to .... these stupid mistakes?

4 With its thatched cottages and pretty gardens,

Minstead is such a .... village.

5 This .... perfume, distilled from oils made in India, costs only £39 a bottle.

3 Write about your town or country, like this:

most frequently/visit: Carthage is the ruin most frequently visited in Tunisia.

1 most well/know ....

....

2 most frequently/write about ....

....

3 most often/talk about ....

....

4 most often/photograph ....

....

5 most/visit ....

....

4 Write about your own country, or any other country, using *to which, from which, through which* or *in which,* like this:

Tunis is a town from which you can go to many places.

5 A friend is going to spend a holiday in a country you know well. Write a paragraph suggesting an itinerary, using the words and phrases below:

you should visit   you really must see   you should go to   it would be a pity if you didn't see   if you have time   then   after that

6 Here are some places and things in a British town. Use your dictionary to make sure you know them all.

traffic lights   roundabout   square   avenue   zebra crossing   pedestrian precinct   recreation ground park   shopping centre/mall   multi-storey car park town hall   courts   public conveniences

Now write five sentences about six of the above using the phrases *at which, in which, from which,* like this:

A pedestrian precinct is a street in which no traffic is allowed.

7 Join the following pairs of sentences, using *to,* like this:

She went to the Post Office. She bought some stamps.
She went to the Post Office to buy some stamps.

1 They used the Porsche. They got there quickly.

....

2 Seat belts are installed. They ensure safe travel.

....

3 After the lesson, Cathy saw the teacher. She explained why she hadn't done the homework.

....

4 Some men stayed on the walls. They guarded the city.

....

5 The Sheriff locked him in the jail. This protected him from the angry crowd.

....

8 Describe a place or a town you know well in your country. Make sure you say where it is situated, how you can get there, and what is interesting about it.

15

Art at the centre

1 Complete these words:

ama＿＿＿r;   cul＿＿＿al;

ar＿＿＿tect＿＿al;

resi＿＿＿＿ia＿;   fle＿＿bl＿

2 Now use the words above in these sentences:

1 I like Paris because of all the . . . . opportunities.

2 Some of the . . . . designs are quite amazing.

3 A good plan is always . . . . because situations can change.

4 No, it's not a . . . . area. It's a commercial centre.

5 Some . . . . football players have a very high standard.

3 Make negative questions, like this:

is/that your brother?: *Isn't that your brother?*

1 was/that Maria? . . . .

. . . .

2 did/you come yesterday? . . . .

. . . .

3 should it be done today? . . . .

. . . .

4 have/you finished it yet? . . . .

. . . .

5 do/you have to go now? . . . .

. . . .

4 Say what the following *must* or *should be able to* do, like this:

A secretary must be able to type.
A secretary should be able to remember appointments.

1 a policeman . . . .

. . . .

2 a pilot . . . .

. . . .

3 a teacher . . . .

. . . .

4 a politician . . . .

. . . .

5 an olympic swimmer . . . .

. . . .

6 a guide dog (for the blind) . . . .

. . . .

7 a good library . . . .

. . . .

8 an arts centre . . . .

. . . .

16

5 Write two or three sentences about a visit to two of the following. Say what you saw, and what you did. Give your opinion about the place.

a museum   an art gallery   a sports centre
a shopping centre   a new city centre

Scenes from Greece

1 Complete these words:

fam___ar; ru__s;

resp____ible;

sig___; inter_____

2 Now use the words above in these sentences:

1 In some parts of Africa the elephant is a common . . . .

2 Parents are . . . . . . for their children

3 Have you ever seen the . . . . . . of ancient Greece?

4 He travels to Greece a lot and so is . . . . . . with their customs.

5 Good news! Joanne has an . . . . . . for a job next week.

3 Change the following sentences using *because of* and *as a result of*, like this:

As he was an excellent photographer, he won the competition.
He won the competition because of his excellent photography.
As a result of his excellent photography, he won the competition.

1 Since she spoke good English, she got the job.

....

....

2 Some people do not support boxing as it can be dangerous.

....

....

3 As the quality of the television programmes is so poor, many people do not watch it.

....

....

4 Since she had a bad cold, she didn't go to work.

....

....

5 As the beaches are so fine, many people go there on holiday.

....

6 Since her father objected, she can't see that film.

....

....

4 Imagine you are a tourist officer in your town. Of course there are some questions you are always being asked. Write five sentences about things that you are always being asked, like this:

I'm always being asked where people can stay.

5 You are on holiday with a friend. Write a postcard to a relative, giving the following information:

where you are staying
the weather
anything interesting you have done
the food

6 You live in a seaside resort. Every year thousands of visitors come to your town. Write five sentences about things that have changed as a result of tourism, using the following expressions:

as a result of   because of   due to   owing to   as a consequence of

17

Dreamer or insomniac?

1 Rearrange these letters to make words from unit 9:

fanstacit .... suignma .... radip

.... cplomtee .... syblmico ....

2 Now use the words above in these sentences:

1 We all laughed a lot. It was one of the most .... plays I've seen.

2 Some dreams are about everyday events. Others are ....

3 Thank you very much. We had a .... time.

4 The train is very .... The journey only takes about two hours.

5 When you .... the form, don't forget to sign.

3 A friend has just visited the UK for the first time. Write about him/her using the expressions below, like this:

She found it necessary to take sleeping pills.

It was He/She found it	possible to ....
	impossible to ....
	necessary to ....
	difficult to....................................
	easy to ....

4 Write suggestions to explain the following situations, using *might have* or *might not have*, like this:

Peter hasn't arrived yet. *He might have missed his train.*

1 Mary didn't phone this morning.

2 I didn't get your letter.

3 He didn't get to work on time.

4 We didn't see them at the football match.

5 She was rushed off suddenly to hospital.

5 Make sentences, following the example:

Horses/cows: *Like horses, cows have tails.*

1 the Austrians/many Swiss

2 birds/bats

3 fish/penguins

4 humans/many animals

5 children/many adults

6 Now finish these sentences in your own words, like this:

Unlike children, adults . . .: *Unlike children, adults have a lot of worries.*

1 Unlike me, my brother/sister/cousin ....

2 Unlike the town in which I live, (name of town) is

3 Unlike the part of the country in which I live,

(another part of your country) is ....

4 Unlike chickens, ...

5 Unlike you, ...

7 Complete this account of a dream in your own words. Write three or four sentences.

I was walking down a street in a strange town. It was dark. The moon was full, but the sky was full of clouds. The buildings seemed to be empty, and I could hear my footsteps echoing on the pavement as I walked. I was frightened, because only a few seconds before I had been with my sister. We had been walking together, and talking about our mother; but she wasn't with me any longer. And I became more frightened.

....

....

....

....

8 Without looking at the text in the Coursebook, rearrange these sentences into the correct order:

1 His manager and a priest assured him that dreams did not come true. . . .

2 One dream that sadly came true, despite the dreamer's efforts to stop the event, happened in 1947. . . .

3 On that occasion they were wrong. . . .

4 Just before a fight a professional boxer dreamt that one of his punches killed his opponent. . . .

Next stop terminal 4

1 Match as many airports from column **A** as you can with the cities in column **B**, and write sentences about them, like this:

I know that . . . . is in . . . . . .

I'm not sure about . . . ., but I think it's the airport

for . . . . . .

I've been to . . . . . . in . . . . . . and in my opinion it's

. . . .

	A	B
1	Dum Dum	Oslo
2	Kennedy	Paris
3	LAX	Delhi
4	Fornebu	Calcutta
5	Kai Tak	Stockholm
6	Heathrow	New York
7	Leonardo da Vinci	London
8	Charles de Gaulle	Los Angeles
9	Palam	Hong Kong
10	Arlanda	Rome

2 Choose as many airlines as you know or can find out about from the list below and say which country they belong to, like this:

TWA is an American airline.
TAP is the national airline of Portugal.

1 Varig ....

....

2 Sabena ....

....

3 SAS ....

....

4 KLM ....

....

5 CP ....

3 Here are some places you might find in and around airports. What happens at each place? Write complete sentences, like this:

Passport control is where you show your passport before entering a country.

1 newsstand ....

....

2 moving walkway ....

....

3 check in ....

....

4 security check ....

....

5 departure gate ....

....

6 control tower ....

....

4 You are in the middle of a transatlantic flight. Write a postcard to a friend telling them about the last few hours.

5 Who do you think might say the following to you?

1 How much luggage do you have? . . . .

2 Are you a smoker or non smoker? . . . .

3 We are now flying at 9,000 metres. . . . .

4 Can I get you anything? . . . .

5 Please extinguish all cigarettes. . . . .

6 Would you put your seat in an upright position.

. . . .

7 What currency would you like? . . . .

19

TAPESCRIPT

1

8 You know, for years the English tried to kill the Welsh language. We weren't allowed to use it, not even at home, and children were encouraged to tell the authorities if their parents were using it. Well, things are changing now. We have our own Welsh language schools, and even a Welsh language university, but a lot more needs to be done. I'm not saying we would like to speak Welsh only. I'm not saying that at all. I'm saying there's a place for Welsh as well as English.

9 John, you were telling me that you are sorry about many things that didn't happen when you were younger. For example, I think you said that if you'd been taught better you'd have gone to university?
–Yes, I think that's fair. And if I'd learnt another language, French for example, then maybe I would have a better and more interesting job. And I've always thought that if I'd studied more at home when I was seventeen and eighteen, instead of having to earn money, it's likely that I'd be a happier person, more confident.

2

7 Listen to each conversation and fill in the chart.
1 Hello, John. Going somewhere?
–Just to the shops. Mary's ill.
Oh, I'm sorry about that. Nothing serious I hope?
–Don't know, really. Hope not. The children are at home and I've got the dinner to cook, too.
2 Ah, Mr Peters, come in.
– Thank you very much.
Take a seat, will you?
–Thank you.
3 Excuse me, Mr Brown.
–Yes, Diana. What is it?
Could you check this letter for me, please?

4 Excuse me, but I wonder if I could open the window.
–Yes, of course. It's terribly hot, isn't it?
Yes, awful. There. That's better. Thank you very much.
5 Where's he gone?
–Don't know. Out somewhere, I expect.
Any idea where?
–None at all. Like a coffee?
6 Are you ready to start now?
–Yes, I think so. What do you want to do first?
Well, I thought we could start with the windows.
–Yes. That's fine.

3

6 1 Mary, I'm going to have a cup of tea. Would you like one?
–Oh yes, please. That would be wonderful.
2 What about something more, John? A little meat, perhaps. There are a lot of vegetables too.
–No thanks. I couldn't really. But it was very good.
Come on. Just a little more. Mary will be very upset if there's any left.

9 1 They ate a huge meal, then left about half an hour afterwards, without saying thank you. I've never invited them since that day.
2 Why didn't he ask you out again?
–Well, I'm not sure. Maybe it was because he paid for the meal and the drinks and the cinema. Perhaps I should have offered to pay something?
3 Have you invited your cousin to your wedding?
–No, why should I? She didn't invite me to hers.

4 Did you enjoy the film?

–Well, it seemed quite good, but I didn't stay until the end because I was sitting next to a man who smoked all the time. I couldn't stand it so I left after an hour.

5 You drive in the same direction as Jack. Why don't you give him a lift?

–I did once or twice, but he never offered to pay anything for petrol so I stopped offering.

12

1 I don't really like men to open doors for me, actually. I can do that quite well myself. I can also put my own coat on by myself. I find all this attention from men quite unnecessary, and also quite false. If you ask me what I think of as good manners it is probably something else altogether. I think that when people are thoughtful, then that's good manners. If you're tired at work, for example, and people accept that you're tired, then that's good manners. I don't think it's really just a question of saying *please* or *thank you*, or doing things like opening doors for people.

2 I like to think I'm well mannered. If I find a woman standing in the bus or on the underground, then I'll certainly offer her my seat. Replying quickly to letters and telephone calls. That's a sign of good manners, too. Not speaking when someone else has something to say, there's another sign. Or speaking too long or too loud when no one else is interested. That's bad manners for me.

3 Saying *please* and *thank you*. Not arguing with my mother. Being quiet when grown ups are speaking. Not shouting in front of visitors. Asking mum if she wants help. That's good manners, isn't it?

4 I hate people who walk round the street with those radios turned on so loudly. And people who push on the bus and underground. It's so unnecessary. One young man even sat next to me and lit a cigarette. It was on the bus. He didn't seem to notice, not even when I started coughing. I don't think people are so polite now as when I was young. People are much ruder.

4 8

Interviewer David, I know Madeleine isn't here, but I think you know what we wanted to ask.

David Yes, I think so. Well, we've been married several years now, and I've lived in France for quite a long time, although we live in London now. One of the great advantages is that I feel much more European and less isolated than I did before. I see things from a European point of view and not just an English one. I now speak good French and that has opened up all the benefits of French culture to me. My life is perhaps richer than it would have been. But of course, there are problems. To begin with my French was bad, Madeleine used to get fed up with speaking English and when we used to argue or when she was tired she'd refuse to speak anything but French. That made me mad because I couldn't understand. She'd just sit there and talk to herself in French, and laugh at me. Food was a problem. English food is good, or at least can be good, but Madeleine is a real chauvinist. As far as she's concerned the English don't make good food, and of course they don't make good coffee, and that has been a real problem with my own family – my parents. And she gets fed up with the way the English only talk about the English. She thinks we're insular and live in the last century. Well maybe we do. But I myself think the French are just the same, always going on about French culture. It makes me sick.

Interviewer Peter, I was really surprised to hear how many problems you and Mary Ann have had. I mean, you speak the same language.

Peter No, we don't. American English and the English I speak might sound similar but to begin with we kept realising that we just weren't communicating at all. It's not just a question of different words, or accent or a little bit of different grammar. It's something else. English humour is different. I'd say something I thought was funny. She wouldn't understand. I'd say something else quite ordinary and we'd realise she just didn't have the knowledge or background to understand what I was trying to say. What I felt was important, she didn't. What worried her didn't worry me. Culturally, we're miles apart. She's constantly concerned about performing well, about being best, about putting herself forward. Frankly, that's never worried me. I've always known I'm good, so why bother?

Interviewer Any advantages?

Peter Lots. The Americans are more open, more adventurous, more positive than the English. You're good because you yourself are good, not because your father is or was. I've got a much better understanding of the world.

Part one

Richard	I was out with a friend that evening when Carol came back from Birmingham. Someone I hadn't seen for ages.
Interviewer	She said she was pretty tired.
Richard	She must've been very tired that night. I mean, she travels a lot, doesn't she?
Interviewer	You seem to spend a long time away from each other.
Richard	Yes, I suppose that's right. We do.
Interviewer	Does that bother you?
Richard	Well, she's got her own life, hasn't she?
Interviewer	Doesn't it make things a little difficult, sometimes?
Richard	Yes and no. Maybe if we had children . . .
Interviewer	And if she were able to spend more time with you, would you be glad?

Part two

Interviewer	Mr Dolby, do you mind if we speak a little about you and Katherine?
David	Go ahead.
Interviewer	She didn't say very much about you to us, you see.
David	Well, we weren't together very long. Only about two years. Didn't she tell you?
Interviewer	No, not exactly. It must have been very difficult leaving your family.
David	Yes and no. I miss the little boy. And I missed Katherine as well at first. Well, there was another baby on the way. That was difficult. Of course, for her too. But it was her choice. Not mine.
Interviewer	You mean she wanted you to go?
David	Yes.
Interviewer	What was wrong?
David	We argued a lot. I had a job and when I got home in the evenings nothing was done. Nothing. I had to cook all the meals. Do the cleaning. It was an impossible situation.

A healer is talking about his first experience of healing.

Healer	Since the war, I guess. I wouldn't have known I could heal unless I'd done it in the war. I wouldn't have believed it could work unless I'd done it myself.
Healer	No, my own experience of healing was spontaneous. No one had taught me anything about it. It just happened. It began during the war. It was at the time of the French campaign of May 1940 and it happened because there were no medical facilities to speak of in my unit. I was horrified that men were being wounded and we had no anaesthetics or trained doctors or nurses, and I felt that I had to put my hands on them, to comfort them. I didn't even think about what I was doing. It must have been because there wasn't time.
Healer	No, it was really only later on that I realised what had happened and I felt real surprise.
Healer	I had stopped severe bleeding and also, because we had no morphine for the pain, when I had put a hand, or two if I could spare them, on a man, the pain began to go away immediately.
Healer	Well, I've asked some of them and I discovered that the people I was treating could feel a variety of things. Most people experienced a change in temperature. Normally they felt a great heat, but sometimes they would tell me they had felt a great cold, almost as if a cold wind was blowing on the area I was touching. Others felt a tingling feeling, like pins and needles, or a feeling of great pressure.
Healer	Yes, they can. Some healers can feel in their hands what is going on. Others feel what is happening by feeling the pain or illness in their own bodies.
Healer	Yes, it has happened to me, actually. It can be rather embarrassing if you are sitting at a dinner party and you develop a very painful knee or an appalling headache which you may be picking up from the person next to you.

A woman is describing what happened to her son.

Interviewer	You've had a lot of problems with your son, haven't you?
Woman	Yes, I have. Just over two years ago Robert started to behave much worse than he had done in the past. He used to be quite a happy boy, but he started to get angry very quickly and for no reason. He screamed a lot. He shouted. Sometimes he seemed to have trouble breathing and sometimes I just couldn't talk to him. It was impossible. Then, on other occasions he would become very quiet, and wouldn't talk. Not even to me. Or his father.
Interviewer	So what did you do?

Woman   So we went to the doctor, and to his school, but despite all the checks that were made there didn't seem to be anything we could do about it. Finally, the doctor said that he might be allergic to certain additives and he might've eaten some food which contains them. So, he suggested a special diet, which cut out all the kinds of food he was used to. That meant no sweets, of course, no ice cream, biscuits, cakes, jams, and also some kinds of meat. The amazing thing is, that by the end of this month he will have been on the diet for a year, and he won't have had any of those behaviour problems in that time. He's completely changed.

Interviewer   You really think it might've been the additives?

Woman   I've got to believe it's the additives, haven't I? I don't know which ones as the doctor never told me, but a friend of mine said she thought the main problem might have been E 102, which does cause breathing problems.

Interviewer   And what now?

Woman   Well, Robert will have to continue on the diet. I might have worried too much about him before, but I certainly don't want to experience it again.

8 7

A representative of an ecological organisation is talking about the advantages and benefits for humans of the rainforests.

1   Four out of five of all children who got leukemia in 1960 died. Now four out of every five survive. The secret of this miraculous change is the rosy periwinkle, a forest flower which tribal doctors had used for centuries.

2   The United States National Cancer Institute has identified more than 2,000 tropical rainforest plants with ability to fight cancer. In fact, about 40% of all drugs given out in the United States today owe much of their strength to chemicals from wildlife, largely from the rainforest.

3   Other drugs include quinine, which comes from a South American tree, and sufferers from high blood pressure get relief from the snakeroot plant from Indian forests. The armadillo, of South America, is helping us find a cure for leprosy.

4   The tropical forests also contain large amounts of new foods. For example, the winged bean of New Guinea is now grown in about 50 different countries. Japanese scientists have found a calorie-free substance in Paraguay which is 300 times sweeter than sugar, and a coffee free of caffeine has been found in the small forests of the Comoros islands.

5   Every day we use products from the rainforests – rubber, spices and oils, and of course trees. Less than one per cent of the forest plants have been examined for their potential, but the remaining 99% is threatened by our endless search for wood. The South American Indians say the trees hold up the sky, and if they come down there will be a catastrophe.

9 10

Norway has decided to resume a 'softly, softly' approach to Britain in the long-standing dispute over the issue of acid rain, as Mrs Rakel Surlien, the Norwegian Minister of the Environment, begins a three-day visit to Britain.

All the Nordic countries believe that Britain is responsible for as much as a third of the acid deposit falling in southern Scandinavia, killing fish and most other aquatic life in thousands of lakes and rivers and possibly putting large areas of forest at risk. Emissions from coal and oil burning power stations are blamed mostly, but Britain insists the case against acid rain in general and its contribution in particular is far from proven.

The issue has become almost fashionable since the Swedes raised it in 1972. More than 20 nations have agreed to join the so-called 30 per cent club, committed to reducing sulphur dioxide by a third, and Britain is increasingly isolated in Western Europe by its refusal to do so.

Mrs Surlien says there has been no change in the Norwegian position in spite of the cordial approach, and she also scents victory, as she said: 'I don't see you can remain isolated in this way for long. It must be very difficult to live with.'

10 9

Interviewer   Right, we're going to be asking some questions about, well, some of the things you read quite a lot about in newspapers these days. Maria, if I can start with you. What do you feel about the exploration of space? Do you feel it's a waste of time?

Maria   Yes, it's a waste of time and money. We've got too many problems down here on earth. I don't think . . .

Juan	I can't agree with you, Maria. The human race has got to explore. It's a fundamental instinct. We always need new frontiers.
Interviewer	OK, Juan, Let's see what you feel about two topics which are more down to earth. Two sea animals. A lot of people today think that whales shouldn't be hunted. They say that their numbers are decreasing, and that many species are in danger of becoming extinct. Just hold on a minute. The other point is also about whales and dolphins. There are many people who feel they shouldn't be kept in captivity. What do you think?
Juan	Well, there are lots of people who think that no animals should be kept in captivity. I myself disagree completely. Keeping animals captive allows us to observe them, and zoos and marinas for dolphins are ideal for allowing the maximum number of people to observe and learn – not just the scientists. As for hunting whales, well I think I would agree that it's unnecessary. What do you think, Maria?
Maria	Absolutely. I think hunting whales should be forbidden. But I'm afraid I'm also one of those who doesn't like to see animals in captivity. And that includes dolphins and whales.

11 [4]

Peter Tyack describes what it is like to be in the water with a humpback whale.
When you get into the water near a singing humpback whale, it can be a scary experience. Your lungs resonate with the sound; it's very loud and you feel it throughout your body – you feel it more than hear it – it's a bit frightening to be sitting thirty feet below the water just having your body reverberate with the sound of a whale. Occasionally one of us is alone in a boat and when he's been out there for a few hours, he'll notice the whale next to the boat, ten or fifteen feet away. One day, sitting alone in the boat, I felt I was being watched. A whale had surfaced and come right up within inches of the boat itself. It looked the boat over and stayed for nearly half an hour. It was hopping and lifting its head up to look into the boat, trying to see. It is very strange to have your wild animal come up to you when you don't expect it.

12 [4]

Interviewer	Edmund Barclay is being interviewed on the radio about his approach to design. What is your overall approach to design?
Edmund Barclay	Do you mean what am I trying to do? Well, as a designer, I firmly believe that good design is a duty; I also feel that the consumer should demand good design. Too many people accept less because they can't afford more. That's nonsense.
Interviewer	Are you saying that good design doesn't have to be expensive?
Edmund Barclay	Exactly. We want to educate the public. We want to give them good products at prices they can afford. We want them to demand better quality.
Interviewer	But surely good design is a matter of taste. What is your definition?
Edmund Barclay	I'm interested in products which look good, are long lasting, and do the job. All three. I think good design is clean and simple. It often uses natural materials, natural woods and fibres, for example, and simple lines. Many of the most beautiful things are designed to be useful – take Mexican pottery, for example, or copper cookware.
Interviewer	Yes, and basketware, or Kashmiri blankets.
Edmund Barclay	Absolutely. And as far as personal taste goes, I think the word we want is appropriate. Does the product suit the particular person? I want people to wear the clothes that suit them; live in rooms that suit their needs. I wouldn't put a family with children into a house full of antiques; I wouldn't put an antique collector into a modern flat.
Interviewer	So you want to please everyone?
Edmund Barclay	We can certainly try.

13 [8]

Interviewer	Judy is answering questions about her life with Gerald. Isn't all this a little strange, living here like this?
Judy	Yes, I expect you <u>do</u> think it's strange. Gerald doesn't have a job. Oh, he does something now and again, you know, like helping a neighbour put up a wall, or repair a car. He's very good with his hands. But in some ways we're like lots of other people. There are millions of people without jobs. We get money from social security, just like they do. In fact, I get my money tomorrow. Anyway, we've got five children, and we teach them at home; we didn't want them to go to school.
Interviewer	But do you think it's right to take money from the state. I mean Gerald could work, couldn't he? I mean, he <u>is</u> very . . .
Judy	That's not the point. We're doing it mainly for the children. We didn't want them to learn, you know, bad habits.

Interviewer	Oh yes, the children. We haven't seen them yet.
Judy	Yes, they're with Gerald, working. The little one's asleep.
Interviewer	You mean they're working on the house or . . .
Judy	No. At their studies.
Interviewer	Can I just talk about the kitchen? Wouldn't you like a washing machine? I mean, with five children it must be . . .
Judy	Yes. Well, he didn't want it. He wouldn't let me.

14 5

Anna and Jay are talking about some of the festivals they have visited.

Anna *Onam* takes place in late August or September in Kerala. That's in the south of the country. This is a harvest festival and the most exciting activities are the many different boat races. *Holi* is very different. It takes place in February or March and it celebrates the beginning of spring. A lot of coloured water – usually red – is thrown around on this occasion, and I've known people who've had to change their clothes several times during the day.

Jay *Songkran* is the old Thai New Year, usually between 13th and 15th April. It's wonderful in the north, around Chiengmai, but everywhere a lot of water is thrown about – on people in particular. In addition, there is a lot of music and dancing. *Songkran* is a festival of boat races, parades and fun fairs as well. I certainly had a fantastic time. The Rocket festival in the north east of Thailand takes place in May, and it is an occasion when the people ask for rain. Here too there's a lot of music and dancing, and of course the rockets, some of them enormous, which are made from bamboo. When these are sent into the sky there is a great deal of noise and music.

7

Berit Andersson is giving a radio interview about festivals in the West.

Interviewer	What is meant by Lucia? What happens?
Berit	She is a girl in a white dress and she wears a crown of candles. They can be electric, of course. Normally today you use batteries because candles can be dangerous, but on special occasions you do find crowns with real candles.
Interviewer	That must be fantastic.
Berit	Yes, it is. She looks like someone from a fairy story.
Interviewer	And when do you see the Lucia?
Berit	Normally she comes very early in the morning. She sings when she comes. Besides her there are other girls carrying candles and wearing white dresses. As well as this they have glitter in their hair and around their waists too.
Interviewer	And they come into the house?
Berit	Yes.
Interviewer	Where from?
Berit	Well, it might be your neighbours, and you might go to your neighbours too. Let me tell you about when I was a little girl. I remember waking early in the morning when my relatives came to us. There was a Lucia, and they had a tray with them, and also special buns and ginger biscuits. In addition, and I remember it very well, there was some mulled wine, because as you can imagine at that time of year it's very cold in Sweden. All this was about six o'clock in the morning. I remember them singing, too. It's a special song which is sung – about the longest day of the year, because that's what Lucia celebrates and perhaps Lucia is also a symbol of light and hope – something we need very much in those dark days.

15 3

Someone is enquiring about the Tunisian holiday.

Agent	Hello, Bath Travel.
Client	Hello, I'd like to find out more about your Tunisian holiday for amateur archaeologists. I've read about it in the paper, but I'd like to know more about what is involved.
Agent	You mean you'd like to know the itinerary?
Client	Yes, that's right.
Agent	All right. Just briefly, you arrive in Tunis at midday on the first day and go by coach to La Marsa. Then there is a short briefing by the archaeologist and then the rest of the day you are free to explore.
	The second day you get up before dawn and go to Carthage to see the sunrise. You have breakfast and a lecture there and then go by coach to Mansoura, where there are beautiful coves. After lunch you can walk along the beach, to Kerkouane. The walk takes about four hours. Kerkouane is one of the most recent and most exciting sites. Then by coach to Kelibia, that's a fishing village, in time for sunset over the harbour.

Client	That sounds rather a long walk.
Agent	Well, it's an easy walk. Flat all the way, and very pretty. But you can go by coach, if you prefer. The third day you spend in Hammamet on Cap Bon, and the day is free to enjoy the town. It's a lovely old town and resort. And the fourth day you take the coach to the ruin of El Djem, which is a magnificent amphitheatre. You have lunch in Sfax and then you take the ferry to the beautiful Kerkenna Islands.
Client	Islands, did you say?
Agent	Yes, they're very peaceful and you spend the fifth day there. The fishermen will take everyone out on their sailing boats and there will be a fishermen's picnic. On the sixth day you visit the Great Mosque of Kairouan and have a picnic lunch. Then take the coach to the lovely port of Bizerte for the last night. And the final day there is a visit to the ancient Roman capital of Utica with its fantastic mosaics and then a coach to Tunis International Airport.
Client	Have you got a full brochure which gives more details?

7

A Tunisian guide at El Djem is describing a Roman circus.

Roman rulers used to give their urban subjects circus shows to keep them happy. At each end of the arena was a royal box where the sponsor could watch and stop the show if necessary. There was a box at each end so that they could be comfortable whatever the season. If the gladiator was defeated he would lie on his back and raise his left arm for forgiveness. But it wasn't always given to him. If the crowd thought he had been courageous they would give the thumbs up sign, but the official in the royal box made the final decision. If he disagreed his thumb was pointed down, and the victim was killed on the spot.

The only disadvantage of the shows was the fact that the crowd wanted more and more, and the shows became more and more brutal. Wild animals would fight gladiators or each other. And sometimes unarmed victims would be thrown to them. Most gladiators were prisoners or criminals, or even people who were bankrupt. These people were on a contract which would pay off their debts – if they weren't killed. Gladiators were very popular and they had their own fan clubs. The most worrying thing about all of this is that it wouldn't have happened unless people wanted it. This really was mass popular entertainment – everyone enjoyed it.

16 | 2

Part one

Man	Isn't the LSO playing at the Barbican on Friday night?
Woman	Yes, I believe it is. Rodriguez' Guitar Concerto, isn't it?
Man	Yes, and Beethoven, I believe. I think I'll ring the booking office tomorrow. Wouldn't you like to come with me?
Woman	Actually, I'd rather go to the Barbican cinema. They're showing Eisenstein's *Ten Days That Shook the World* and Friday's the last night.
Man	Oh, won't you come with me? I really don't want to go alone.
Woman	Yes, I suppose so, but I'd rather not. Couldn't you learn to be more independent?

Part two

1	Isn't that the Pompidou Centre over there?	4	Isn't it better to go on Saturday when it isn't so crowded?
2	Wouldn't you like to come to the Barbican with me?	5	Couldn't we go a bit sooner than that?
3	Isn't the cafeteria better than the restaurant?	6	That isn't the Barbican, is it?
		7	Couldn't you be a bit more flexible?

7

The Pompidou Centre has become the most controversial building in Paris – people either love it or hate it. Its critics wonder if such modern architecture should be among the stone walls of such an old historical neighbourhood. And yet the building of the Centre has brought the Beaubourg district back to life. Without it the entire quarter might have been pulled down.

The centre isn't a closed museum, but an open, living structure. All the parts which are usually hidden inside a building are exposed – on the outside. All the services are colour-coded and this makes people want to understand the building's metabolism – how it works. The main structural skeleton is white, and all the other colours show important services, which keep the building alive. Red is for vertical transportation, such as lifts and escalators, green for water, blue for air-conditioning and yellow for electricity. It is like a human body with all its organs and systems outside, including the skeleton.

Each level is a bridge supported by columns and balanced by a system of flexible arms. The floors inside are based on the same system, and this allows them to be lifted or lowered. The centre has been built so that it can be changed completely inside: the size of its rooms, its walls and floor heights.

One of the unique features of the Piano-Rogers design is the enormous open carnival square in front of the building, as large as the space occupied by the building itself. The plaza, which slopes gently and is paved with cobblestones, is everyone's stage: you may see a single acrobat or a fire-eater, a lonely musician or a full orchestra. The escalator is outside the main structure and inside a transparent tube, and it's been compared to a roller coaster. It takes visitors to every floor, but they can see everything that is happening below, in the public square and nearby. At the top there is a breathtaking view of Paris and you can see Notre Dame and the Tour St Jacques, the Eiffel Tower and the Sacré Coeur.

17 | 4

Takis is describing one of his postcards.

Takis   I try to put on the paper some scenes from everyday life, some thoughts from my head, or some parts of book or poems I have read. This one, for instance, is a cup of coffee and an old man. It was my cup of coffee, actually. The man is five or six metres away. And I tried to show a Greek breakfast – at least my idea of a Greek breakfast. The Greek breakfast consists of a small cup of coffee like that, and five or six cigarettes. The picture's taken using slow film, a special lens and a filter, which means that half of the picture's close up and the other half isn't. The camera focuses on two different distances: on my cup of coffee – eight or ten inches from the camera, and then on the old man – five or six metres away. So the cup of coffee looks larger. And I've left the top of the glass out of focus, on purpose, so that it looks like the water is very cold.

Interviewer   Did the man know he was being photographed?

Takis   No, the man was surprised. He was watching me. But as I had the camera under the table, he didn't know what I was doing. I moved the cup of coffee forward and backward so it would be in focus, you see. And then he wondered: 'What is he doing with that?' And then I took the photograph.

6

Takis is describing how he chooses his subjects.

Interviewer   Do you recognise a photograph you want to take straight away?

Takis   Sometimes, I don't. For example here. I saw the cat. Also, I saw the bars, but I passed by. Some seconds later I realised that I wanted it. Cats can't be in jail. But would she still be there? Why should she wait for me? I tried it anyway and she was there, waiting.

Interviewer   What made you take that one?

Takis   I saw some flowers and some curves, light pink colour. Besides this I saw two hearts. And I liked it. I felt something in my throat like I had to swallow something and couldn't. Then I wondered: 'Am I jealous now?' Everybody can see that the people who made that sign were in love.

Interviewer   And where is this?

Takis   This taverna is close to my home. People were having a party there. And I wanted to take a picture. Behind the musicians there was a mirror. Since there were too many reflections of people in the mirror, I used a filter. In addition to this I wanted to make the edge of the picture milky. I waited there until the reflections of some of the people who were dancing appeared in the mirror. And then I took it.

Interviewer   This one fascinates me.

Takis   It's a door, and the yard of a house. As well as this you have the sea in the background, and the sky. Behind that door is a garden. This gate is so beautiful. I liked it. I had to do something special, to show exactly what the subject was like. I had to do something – something like painting, for example, which leaves out or puts in some more things. I did it like that.

Interviewer   It certainly looks like a painting.

Takis   That's what I wanted.

Interviewer   What about the one with the green railing?

Takis   This is a scene from a Greek island and on this island everything is white. When I think of the sea, I always think of something white as well. White walls, for example, or white birds, white foam on the waves. Blue cannot just be plain blue. There has to be something white. So I took a picture with just white walls and nothing else, and just the green railing there. And a bit of light blue sky.